THE PRINCIPLES OF

INVENTORY

MANAGEMENT

BY ARTHUR SNYDER

ISBN: I-4196-7272-X

Library of Congress Control Number: 2007905153

Publisher: BookSurge Publishing

North Charleston, South Carolina

Table Of Contents

THE PRINCIPLES OF INVENTORY MANAGEMENT

Foreword

In April 1963, my father, Arthur Snyder, published The Principles of Inventory Management. It was the fruit of his work on inventory management while at Norton Company, Worcester, Mass. He began there as an engineer in 1952, rising to controller & treasurer for Behr-Manning, Troy, N.Y., a Norton affiliate. The first run of this book was 2,000 copies; most were distributed to manufacturing customers and within the Norton organization.

This book received a boost in April 1964 when Financial Executive magazine published a condensed version. That publishing garnered feedback from around the world, sparking an update published in Financial Executive in September 1964; that update is included in this edition.

Arthur Snyder left Norton in 1965, but the book's influence continued through the 1970s and beyond, often quoted in scholarly articles, letters and books by those who specialized in this discipline. For example:

- A letter from Walter R. Crowe of Lakehead University in Thunder Bay, Ontario, Canada published in the Summer 1971 edition of Operations Research magazine likened my father's model and other models to the Harris EOQ/lot-size expression.

- An article by Richard L. Meyer and Fred B. Power in the December 1973 edition of The Journal of Risk and Insurance, entitled "Total Insurance Costs and the Frequency of Premium Payments," presented a variation on my father's model to enable a policyholder to select the correct number of payments to minimize his or her total real insurance costs.

We are republishing this book to keep alive this contribution to the principles of inventory management, which -- despite advances in technology -- remain consistent.

I've also taken great pleasure in furthering a project begun by my father.

After joining A.M. Best Company in 1965, two years later he became the top officer, a position he continues to hold as he guides the world's oldest rating agency into its second century. Despite his career change, I believe he remains an engineer at heart, proud of his accomplishments with the Norton Company.

We would be pleased to field any additional comment. Please send your thoughts to principles@ambest.com.

Arthur Snyder III

THE PRINCIPLES OF INVENTORY MANAGEMENT

Chapter I

Introduction

"Why are we always out of stock?" Behind this question lies one of the most perplexing problems facing businessmen today. They are confronted with the dilemma of attempting to simultaneously (1) meet ever-increasing demands for improved customer service, (2) maintain, stable production operations and (3) keep the investment in inventory at a reasonable level. As a result, during the past decade we have seen a great deal of interest and attention devoted to the subject of inventory management. Unfortunately, considerable doubt and confusion still exist as to — what are the basic tools of inventory control; where do they come from; and how should they be used?

It is the purpose of this study to analyze the development and application of the principles of inventory control. In discussing these techniques, it is often necessary to use concepts and terminologies which might be foreign to many businessmen. It is impossible, however, to acquire a sound knowledge of these principles without becoming familiar with the fundamental tools upon which they are based.

Hundreds of articles have been written on this subject. Unfortunately, very few provide the reader with anything but generalizations. The contents of this study, therefore, should not be looked upon as either an academic exercise in math or as a review of clever clerical devices which can help short-cut the labyrinth of confusion. Properly understood, these concepts will help the businessman make better policy decisions, which in turn will generate more useful and satisfying procedures. As such, these techniques are worth some time and thought, commensurate with the importance of inventory policy in your business operation.

Included is a new theory on economic ordering quantity (EOQ) which shows how the EOQ can be interpreted as a quantity range, rather than a fixed quantity. It is current practice to rigidly adhere to the specific quantity obtained by using the EOQ formula. Deviations from the EOQ are made only under the assumed penalty of increased inventory costs. This "myth" will be exposed and it will be shown that the EOQ can be interpreted as a quantity range imparting flexibility to the production and inventory control system.

RISING INVENTORY COSTS

Before discussing the principles of inventory management, we should briefly review one of the problems we are trying to control — rising inventory costs. During the past decade, there has been a trend towards higher levels of inventory coupled with rising inventory carrying costs. The growth of inventory levels has been caused by three changes in our business environment:

- In many industries, there has been a gradual shifting of the inventory burden carried in the channels of distribution, back towards the manufacturer. In an effort to improve his inventory position, the customer has taken advantage of sales competition by forcing his distributors into carrying his safety stock requirements and providing prompt delivery on special or seldom used items. Naturally, this resulted in a chain reaction through the channels of supply and unfortunately the last link is the manufacturer.

- A second change contributing to higher inventory levels is the trend towards shorter delivery dates. Competitive pressure has forced many companies to comply with a delivery schedule which is considerably shorter than their manufacturing or procurement cycle. Consequently we have witnessed a growth in work-in-process inventories which reflect anticipated sales.

- A third change influencing inventory levels is the intense desire of business management during the past decade to diversify their product lines. The attempt to diversify has ranged from the technological modification of existing products to satisfy a particular market or customer requirement, to the addition of completely new and unfamiliar product lines. Obviously, diversification adds to the problem of inventory control.

In addition to the factors creating a demand for higher levels of inventory, there has been the steady increase in inventory carrying costs. The continual rise in direct costs for space and handling requires no explanation. Indirect costs for taxes, insurance, and obsolescence have increased proportionately.

In summary, the four major factors contributing to the trend towards rising inventory costs have been (1) the shifting of the inventory burden in the channels of distribution back towards the manufacturer, (2) the competitive pressure of improved service and delivery, (3) the desire for product line diversification, and (4) rising inventory carrying costs.

THE SCIENTIFIC APPROACH

The advent of data processing ushered in what may be called a scientific approach to inventory management. Inventory control had long been considered an intuitive process, and responsibility for it was usually vested in men with long experience and a detailed knowledge of the products they controlled. It has been only in recent years that management has recognized and accepted a more scientific approach to inventory control.

Because the approach is termed "scientific" does not imply that computers and advanced mathematics are absolutely necessary in solving inventory problems; experience and sound judgment are still very important elements. The scientific approach does, however, eliminate intuition by recommending that any inventory control procedure be constructed in three phases: Theory — Application — and Policy.

1) *Theory* — An inventory control program is primarily the application of management policy, and its success is dependent on how well these management policies are conceived, communicated, and executed. Before sound management policy decisions can be made, however, the theories upon which inventory control is based must first be understood.

2) *Application* — The second phase involves the development of a specific inventory control system based on the modification of these theories to provide for their practical and economic application. The successful system is designed to serve the particular needs of a company. This requires a thorough knowledge of the cost structure, sales pattern, and competitive market for each product line to be controlled by the inventory procedure.

3) *Policy* — The third, and perhaps most important, phase is a clearly-stated policy from management to all line and staff personnel setting forth what the inventory control policy is and who is responsible for its execution.

In effect, the scientific approach to inventory control is primarily the systematic application of sound management policy coupled with certain fundamentals that were taught in university classrooms more than 20 years ago.

Chapter II

Theories of Inventory Control

As previously mentioned, an inventory control program should progress through three stages of development: theory, application, and policy. The success of the project will depend largely on how well the theories of inventory control are understood by those charged with the responsibility of the program. Particular attention must be given, therefore, to acquiring a thorough knowledge of the three fundamental concepts which form the foundation of any sound inventory control system:

1) Classification   —   What to control.

2) Order Point   —   When to make or buy.

3) Economic Lot Size   —   How much to make or buy.

Let's briefly examine each of these concepts to see how it is derived and adapted to practice.

CLASSIFICATION — WHAT TO CONTROL

The purpose of classification techniques is to provide a means whereby inventory control efforts can be directed toward those areas where they can be most effective. On items of small value, it is seldom justifiable to use the same close and detailed control that is applied to high valued or critical items. If you do, you may be spending more to keep these low-value items within a prescribed limit than a slight excess in inventory might cost or you are stealing time from controlling those items that require close policing.

Studies have shown that the average manufacturing company has an inventory which is distributed as to number of items and dollar value as follows:

Group	No. of Items	Inventory Value
A	15%	70%
B	30%	20%
C	55%	10%
	100%	100%

As shown, Group A contains only 15% of the physical number of items, but represents 70% of the total inventory value. It is logical to assume that the more valuable items merit greater attention. This can be accomplished by giving them an

"A" rating and reviewing these items more often. This system is often referred to as the "ABC Analysis of Inventory."

Other factors, which are just as important as dollar value, to consider when developing a classification plan include: the frequency and quantity of demand for an item, its rate of obsolescence, and whether it is a critical item, the lack of which would create a serious inconvenience to the company or a customer. In short, the development of a sound method of classification and record keeping is the first step towards improved inventory control.

ORDER POINT (OP)

The Order Point (OP) equation is a tool for evaluating the factors affecting the question — "When should I make or buy?" The purpose of the Order Point is to signal when the inventory level of a particular item has reached the point where, based on forecasted usage, it will be completely exhausted during the time required to manufacture or produce a replenishment stock. The equation is:

$$\text{Order Point (OP)} = S(P-L) + F\sqrt{SQ(P-L)}$$

S = Sales or Usage   F = Stockout Acceptance Factor
L = Lead Time   P = Production or Procurement Cycle
Q = Units Per Demand

The definitions of the variables used in the Order Point equation are included in Appendix A and an analysis of the derivation of the equation is given in Appendix B. These schedules should be studied carefully as it is important that the individuals responsible for the development of an inventory control program thoroughly understand the tools they are about to use.

It is the function of the Order Point to optimize the two opposing conditions of minimizing the inventory investment while satisfying demand and reducing the possibility of stockouts to an acceptable level. While in theory it is desirable never to have a stockout, for all practical business applications a certain level of stockouts must be planned for and tolerated. Stockouts are the result of fluctuations in usage from the forecasted level. These fluctuations are intensified for those items which have large variations in their usage (S) or in the average number of units per demand (Q).

In order to allow for these fluctuations in the demand pattern, the Order Point equation provides for the addition of safety stock. The determination of how much safety stock is required to establish an acceptable stockout level is based on the application of a formula known as the "Square Root Approximation of the Poisson

Distribution." Statistical studies have shown that there is an acceptable correlation between the fluctuations in an average industrial demand pattern and the Poisson distribution. If the fluctuations for a given industry or product line are abnormal, the formula will break down under testing and modifications to the value of the Stockout Acceptance Factor (F), as it relates to the percentage of stockouts, will be required. These situations can occasionally be anticipated by testing the Order Point with actual historical data.

Almost every business requires some safety stock; the amount is largely determined by competitive practices and demands of the trade. Weighing the cost of additional inventory against the loss of a sale and customer goodwill is an important inventory policy decision. It is possible to develop a formula which equates (a) the loss resulting from a stockout in terms of either a lost sale and/or customer goodwill to (b) the cost to carry the additional inventory necessary to prevent the stockout. Such a formula, however, has proven to be quite theoretical and impractical. The problems to resolve are: what portion of the safety stock is responsible for the stockout, what percentage of the stockouts result in an actual lost sale, what is the value of customer goodwill, etc. The general practice is, or should be, to establish an OP using tentatively agreed upon safety stock limits and adjust the latter based on experience and desired objectives.

A common mistake made in the administration of the OP is the practice of releasing a stock replenishment order (when the OP is reached) for a lot size as determined by the EOQ without giving consideration as to whether or not the remaining stock balance is significantly below the OP. For example, an item has a current OP of 100 units and an EOQ of 50 units. The present stock balance of 140 units is reduced to 80 units by orders for 60 units. Many inventory systems would trigger off a stock replenishment order of 50 units (instead of 70 units) ignoring that 20 units are needed to restore the stock balance to the OP.

The result is usually frequent stockouts. To correct this situation, the OPs are raised which in turn increase the inventory levels. These factors naturally generate dissatisfaction with the system. The practice of rigidly adhering to the EOQ is based on the assumption that the EOQ is a specific quantity and any deviation will result in increased inventory costs. As will be shown in Chapter III, the EOQ under most conditions can be interpreted as a rather broad quantity range thereby imparting flexibility to the inventory control system.

Another implied condition, but worthy of emphasis, is that the administration of the OP should carefully distinguish between items "in-stock" and items "in-process." Using the previous example, after release of a 70-unit stock replenishment order, the 150 units of stock would be distributed as follows:

80 units in-stock and 70 units in-process. An order for 50 units would reduce the stock balance to the OP and require the release of another stock replenishment order. The number of units in stock, however, has been reduced to a dangerously low level of 30 units and the system should automatically "flag" this condition to permit, if deemed necessary, one of the previous stock orders to be expedited through production to avoid the possibility of a stock-out condition. If possible, all in-process orders should show the date released, or even better, the expected date of completion.

ECONOMIC ORDERING QUANTITY (EOQ)

The determination of order quantities is primarily a matter of economics. By increasing the size of an order we reduce the unit cost because we spread the one-time production and/or procurement costs over a larger number of units. On the other hand, there are factors which argue for limiting the lot size such as: the increased inventory investment, higher inventory carrying charges, and a greater risk of obsolescence and spoiled work.

The economic ordering quantity equation (or EOQ, as it is more frequently called) provides a means whereby the several factors affecting the cost of a unit can be evaluated simultaneously to determine which lot size will generate the lowest unit cost for a given set of conditions. This familiar equation takes the following form.

$$EOQ = \sqrt{\frac{2SO}{RU} + \frac{PSO}{U} - \frac{O}{U}} \cong \sqrt{\frac{2SO}{RU}}$$

S = Sales or Usage   R = Investment Factor
O = Ordering Costs   P = Production or Procurement Cycle
U = Unit Costs

The simplified version of the EOQ formula is sufficiently accurate for most business applications as the last two functions do not significantly contribute to the final value of the EOQ. Appendix E provides EOQ Tables for various values of the variables in the EOQ formula. Production or procurement cycles of 0.5 and 3 months are used to show how the introduction of this variable has very little effect on the final value of the EOQ.

As previously emphasized, the development of a sound inventory control program requires that the responsible individuals be thoroughly familiar with the basic theories involved. By itself, the EOQ formula is meaningless unless we understand the function of the factors it is based upon and what assumptions are used in its derivation. With this in mind, the derivation of the EOQ formula is discussed in Appendix C.

Chapter III

EOQ Range Theory

There are two misconceptions concerning the use of the EOQ formula for determining economic ordering quantities. First, that the EOQ is a specific quantity and, second, that a small deviation from this specific quantity substantially increases the total cost per unit. The implied inflexibility of the EOQ has always been a source of concern to those individuals charged with the responsibility of managing the inventory control system. In actual practice, it is often necessary to release a lot size which is greater or less than the EOQ. These deviations from the EOQ are usually reluctantly approved because it is believed there will be a significant increase in the total unit cost. In this chapter we will show that for all practical purposes the EOQ can be interpreted as a quantity range within which can be realized the minimum total unit cost.

ADVANTAGES OF EOQ RANGE

The ability to interpret the EOQ as a range of quantities, rather than a specific quantity, has many advantages. In general, it imparts flexibility to the inventory and production control system permitting desired adjustments to the ordering quantity without the fear of increased cost. Deviations from the EOQ might be prompted by any one of the following reasons:

Less Than EOQ

The use of ordering quantities less than the EOQ are often prompted by conditions such as: the desire to reduce work-in-process inventory, fear of product obsolescence when the EOQ exceeds more than 6-12 months' supply, conservative adjustment to an optimistic sales forecast, or the desire to smooth out the production load by staggering the release of several small lot sizes.

More Than EOQ

Those situations which pressure for the release of ordering quantities larger than the EOQ are: to permit an adjustment of the production load by providing work during a temporary slack period, to build inventory in lieu of anticipated loss of normal capacity due to material shortages, strike, or heavy vacation periods, or to make-up for shortages between the stock balance and the OP.

Other types of adjustments include the desire to modify the EOQ to utilize the full capacity of a machine or to facilitate handing. What ever the reason may be, there is general agreement that a system which is flexible within controlled limits is preferred over an inflexible system. The latter often creates more problems than it solves.

EOQ FORMULA

The assumption that the EOQ is a specific quantity and any deviation from this quantity increases the total cost per unit stems primarily from the popular concept that cost per unit, plotted as a function of the ordering quantity, results in a curve with a distinct minimum point as shown in Figure #1. The implied unity of the EOQ point is further supported by the EOQ formula which provides only one answer for any given set of data.

Let us direct our attention to Figure #2 which represents an enlargement of the area near the EOQ point in Figure #1. Figure #2 shows that what appeared to be a distinct minimum point in Figure #1 is really a flat portion of the curve which extends on either side of the specific EOQ point. It will be shown that this condition is the rule and not an exception created by the data chosen for the illustration.

Based on the above example and an understanding of the mathematical derivation of the EOQ formula as outlined in Appendix C, two observations can be made: (1) the EOQ is a precisely determined point on the total cost curve, and (2) this curve has an extremely long and flat portion at the theoretical minimum cost (or EOQ) point. What we intend to prove, therefore, is that the EOQ is not a specific point, but a section of the total cost curve. This section represents the economic order quantity range which will provide the same minimum total cost per unit as the specific EOQ.

CASE PROBLEM

To clearly illustrate this point, let us use a case problem choosing fairly representative data for the variables involved. Suppose the XYZ Co. manufactures "Widgets" and the necessary production and inventory control data for this product is as follows:

Symbol	Definition	Value
S	Sales Volume	100 per month
P	Production Cycle	1 Month
O	Ordering Costs	$1.00
U	Unit Cost	$10.00 each
R	Investment Factor	24% per year
L	Lead Time	½ Month
Q	Units per Demand	5
F	Stockout Acceptance	10% (1.29)

FIGURE #1

TOTAL COST CURVE

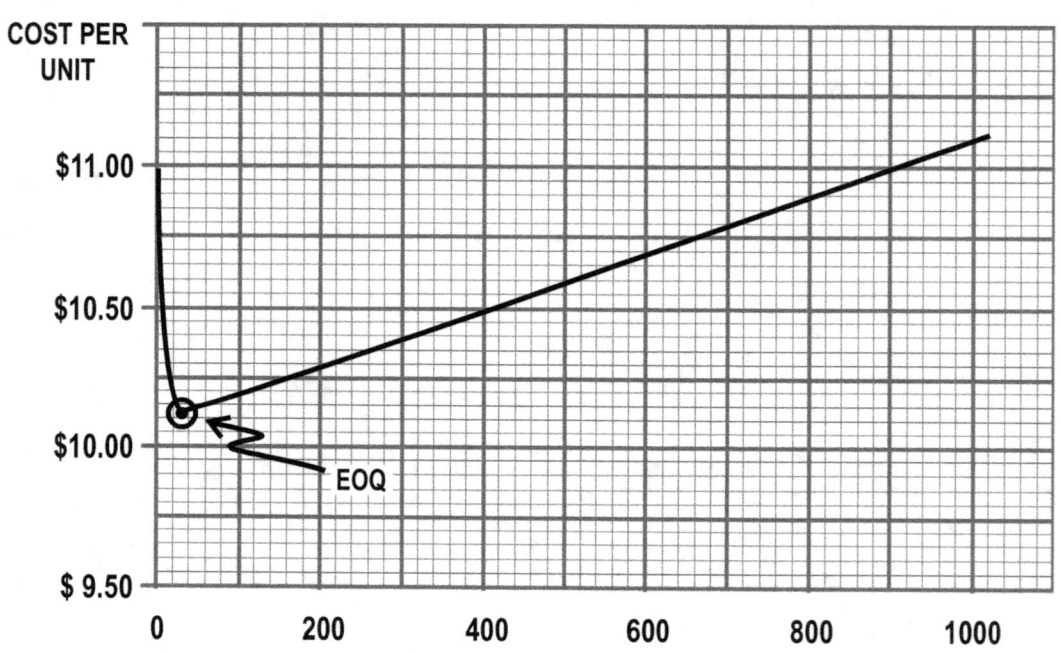

QUANTITY ORDERED (N)

Data based on Case Problem – "Widgets"

FIGURE #2

ENLARGED SECTION OF

TOTAL COST CURVE

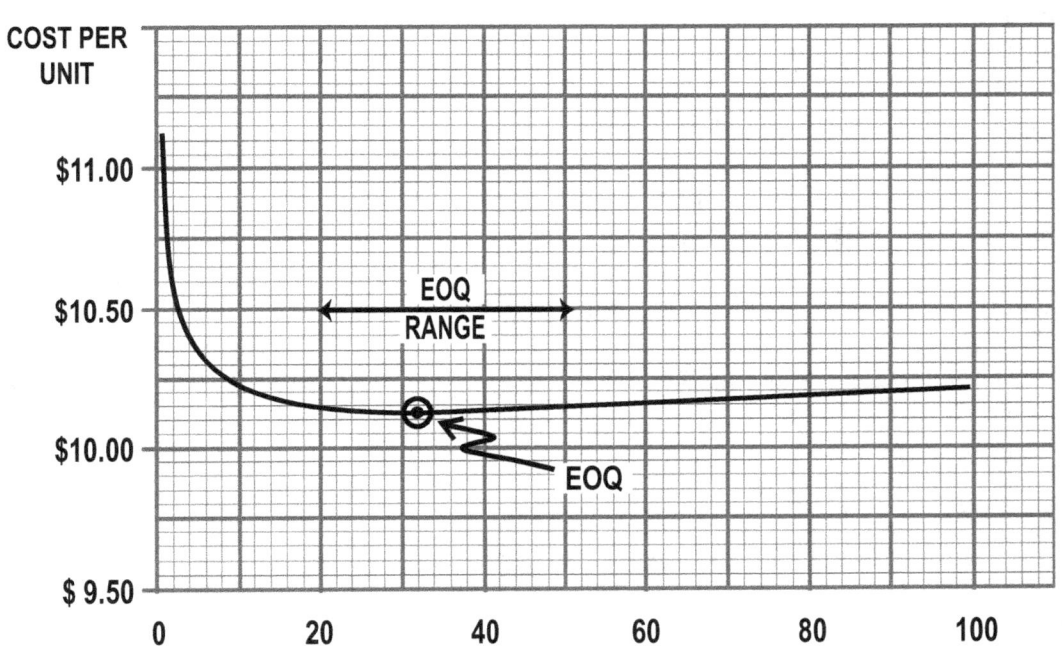

QUANTITY ORDERED (N)

Data based on Case Problem – "Widgets"

Based on the given data and respective formulas developed in Chapter II, the inventory control procedure for this product would be to establish an order point (OP) of 70 units and a lot size (EOQ) of 32 units.

$$OP = S(P-L) + F\sqrt{SQ(P-L)} = 70 \text{ units}$$

$$EOQ = \sqrt{\frac{2SO}{RU}} = 31.6 \text{ units}$$

We are satisfied with the determination of an order point (OP) of 70 units. As explained in Chapter II, the OP is primarily a function of our sales forecast and the production cycle. To the minimum OP of 50 units, we have added a buffer stock of 9 units to reduce the probability of stockout to 10% and 11 units to adjust the OP for the fact that we average 5 units per order. We recognize that the latter may have to be adjusted based on actual experience.

The lot size of 32 is interpreted as the most economic manufacturing quantity based on the given values of S, O, R, and U. It is implied that a deviation from this quantity will result in a significant increase in the total cost per unit. Rather than accepting this statement, let us actually examine the effect on the total unit cost (TUC) as the ordering quantity is increased or decreased from the EOQ of 32 units. The equation for calculating the TUC for a given quantity (N) is derived in Appendix C and shown as follows:

$$TUC = \left[\frac{O}{N} + U\right]\left[1 + \frac{RP}{2} + \frac{RN}{2S} - \frac{R}{2S}\right]$$

Substituting the given data for "Widgets," the total cost per unit as a function of the ordering quantity (N) simplifies to:

$$TUC = \$10.10 + \frac{\$1.01}{N} + \$.001\,N$$

Using the above expression, the total cost per unit for lot sizes from 1 to 1,000 is shown in Figure #3. This data was also used for plotting the graphs shown in Figures #1 and #2.

EOQ VS. COST

In Chapter II and the supporting Appendix C, we discussed the derivation of the EOQ formula. Its function is to provide an answer to the question: "What ordering quantity will generate the minimum total cost per unit?" Using the data chosen for our case problem, the EOQ is calculated as 31.6 units which results in a minimum total cost of $10.16 per unit. If we look at Figure #3, however, we find that this is the minimum cost only if we extend the value to four positions after the

FIGURE #3

CASE PROBLEM

TOTAL UNIT COST

Order Quantity (N)	Total Cost Per Unit	
	Exact	Nearest Cent
1	$11.1101	$11.11
5	10.3061	10.31
10	10.2101	10.21
15	10.1814	10.18
20	10.1696	10.17
25	10.1645	10.16
EOQ = 31.6	10.1627	10.16
40	10.1644	10.16
45	10.1665	10.17
55	10.1725	10.17
60	10.1759	10.18
75	10.1876	10.19
100	10.2092	10.21
200	10.3042	10.30
300	10.4025	10.40
500	10.6011	10.60
1000	11.1001	11.10

decimal or $10.1627. Any lot size between the quantity range of 25-40 has a total variable cost of $10.16 when rounded off to the nearest cent.

This quantity range is not clearly evident if we inspect Figure #1 which represents the universal impression of what the total cost curve looks like. Due to the large quantity range used for the X-axis, the curve appears to have a distinct minimum point or EOQ. As previously discussed, if we enlarge the section of the curve near the EOQ as shown in Figure #2, we readily see what the unit cost figures tell us; the curve near the EOQ point is almost flat. The EOQ is merely the precisely calculated low-point of this flat section. Hence, for most conditions, the EOQ can be considered a range of quantities rather than a specific quantity.

Let us carry these observations to a further conclusion using our case problems for illustration. The management of the XYZ Co. desires to impart flexibility to the ordering quantities of their new product "Widgets." They agree that 32 units is the theoretical quantity that will produce the minimum total cost per unit, but recognize the values of the variables they chose for calculating the EOQ are not necessarily exact. They are willing, therefore, to work within an EOQ range that does not exceed ½ of 1% of the theoretical minimum total cost per unit. An increase of ½ of 1% over the minimum cost of $10.16 would extend the acceptable cost range to $10.21. On this basis, instead of an EOQ of 32 units, sales and production management could gear their operations to the release of lot sizes which vary from 10 to 100 units.

EOQ VS. COST RATIO

The EOQ formula can be thought of as a function of sales volume (S), investment factor (R) and cost (O,U). The equation when separated in this manner appears as follows:

$$EOQ = \sqrt{\frac{2SO}{RU}} = \sqrt{S \times \frac{2}{R} \times \frac{O}{U}}$$

When viewed in this manner, it becomes evident that it is the ratio of ordering to unit costs (O/U), rather than their absolute values, which determines the EOQ. For example, in the case problem we chose a value of $1 for ordering costs and $10 for unit costs giving a ratio of 1:10. For the same values of S and R, any combinations of absolute values for O and U which maintain the same 1:10 ratio will result in the same EOQ, i.e.:

Variable	Examples		
	#1	#2	#3
S (month)	100	100	100
R (year)	24%	24%	24%
O	$1.00	$5.00	$2.20
U	$10.00	$50.00	$22.00
K= O/U	0.1	0.1	0.1
EOQ	32	32	32

It is often difficult to establish accurate and acceptable ordering and unit costs. The interpretation of these costs as a ratio, rather than as individual absolute amounts, can serve as a very useful approach to handling the cost aspect of the EOQ formula. The use of a cost ratio (O/U) establishes the proper relationship between the two costs. For instance, if the unit cost for an item is $22, there is no need to fret over whether the ordering cost is $2.00 or $2.20. The effect on the cost ratio and, hence, the EOQ is insignificant. Further, it often simplifies the problem of how much variable overhead cost should be added to each cost. If overhead is a percentage addition to each cost, then it can be ignored as it will not change the ratio. Another advantage to the cost ratio approach is it permits products with similar cost ratios to be grouped and handled with the same inventory control charts and procedures.

EOQ VS. SALES VOLUME

Under most conditions, once the cost ratio (O/U) and investment factor (R) have been determined and agreed upon for a given product, they can be considered constant unless involved in a major cost change. This reduces, therefore, the EOQ formula to the function of one true variable — sales volume.

In the case problem, we chose a sales volume (S) of 100 units per month and arrived at an EOQ of 32 units and an EOQ Range of 10-100 units for the control limit of ½ of 1% increase in minimum total variable cost. Figure #4 shows the effect on the EOQ and EOQ Range for changes in the sales volume (S) from 1 to 250 units per month. The EOQ was calculated using the standard EOQ formula and the EOQ Range was determined using the expression developed in Appendix D substituting the value T= .005 for the control limit of ½ of 1%. If a control limit of 1/10 of 1% was desired, a value of T = .001 would be used.

Figure #4 shows that for the given data of the case problem, the EOQ Range is significant for all levels of sales volume. When the forecasted sales volume drops to 5 per month, a quantity range of 4 to 13 units provides the same minimum cost as the EOQ of 7. At a forecasted sales volume of 250 units per month, the EOQ is

FIGURE #4

CASE PROBLEM

EOQ RANGE

Sales Volume (S)	EOQ	EOQ Range (+½%)
1	3	2-5
5	7	4-13
10	10	4-20
20	14	6-32
30	17	7-42
50	22	8-61
75	28	9-86
100	32	10-105
250	50	12-214

50 units, but the same minimum cost will be realized for any lot size within the limits of 12 to 214 units. Working within the EOQ Range, the production control manager could stagger the release of lot sizes to fit a daily, weekly, or monthly schedule if such is desired.

APPLICATION OF EOQ RANGE THEORY

At this point, a criticism could be made by the practitioners of production and inventory control that the availability of an EOQ Range complicates the problem as it introduces a decision as to what lot size to use whereas previously the choice was limited to a specific EOQ. If this is a problem, then the solution lies in a well-defined management policy describing the procedure to follow in determining the proper lot size. To explore some of the ways the EOQ Range can be adapted to practice, let us return to our case problem of Widgets.

Figure #5 shows one way in which the EOQ Range, as a function of sales volume, can be represented graphically for easy reference. In a similar manner, Figure #6 shows a graph of the order point as a function of sales volume. The order point is shown with and without the addition of safety stock, the latter being based on a 10% stockout acceptance level. Using these graphs, which could be combined, variations in management policy concerning the inventory control of "Widgets" could be introduced.

1) During the initial stages of introducing the product to the market, the EOQ lot size will be standardized at 20 units. The release of small lot sizes is desired by the factory to minimize spoilage usually associated with a new product and reduce the possibility of building excess inventory in case sales do not reach forecasted volumes. An OP of 50 units will be established which represents the order point for sales (S) of 100 units per month without the addition of safety stock.

2) After the production bugs have been worked out, the EOQ will be increased to 50 units and the OP to 70 units provided the forecasted sales volume and buying pattern materializes.

3) Since this is a seasonal item with peak demand during the fourth quarter, additional inventory will be built in the third quarter by increasing the lot size to the maximum level (105 units for forecasted sales of 100 units per month).

4) As the product matures or obsolescence is feared, the OP could be reduced by eliminating the safety stock and the lot size reduced to 20 units.

FIGURE #5

CASE PROBLEM

EOQ RANGE CURVE

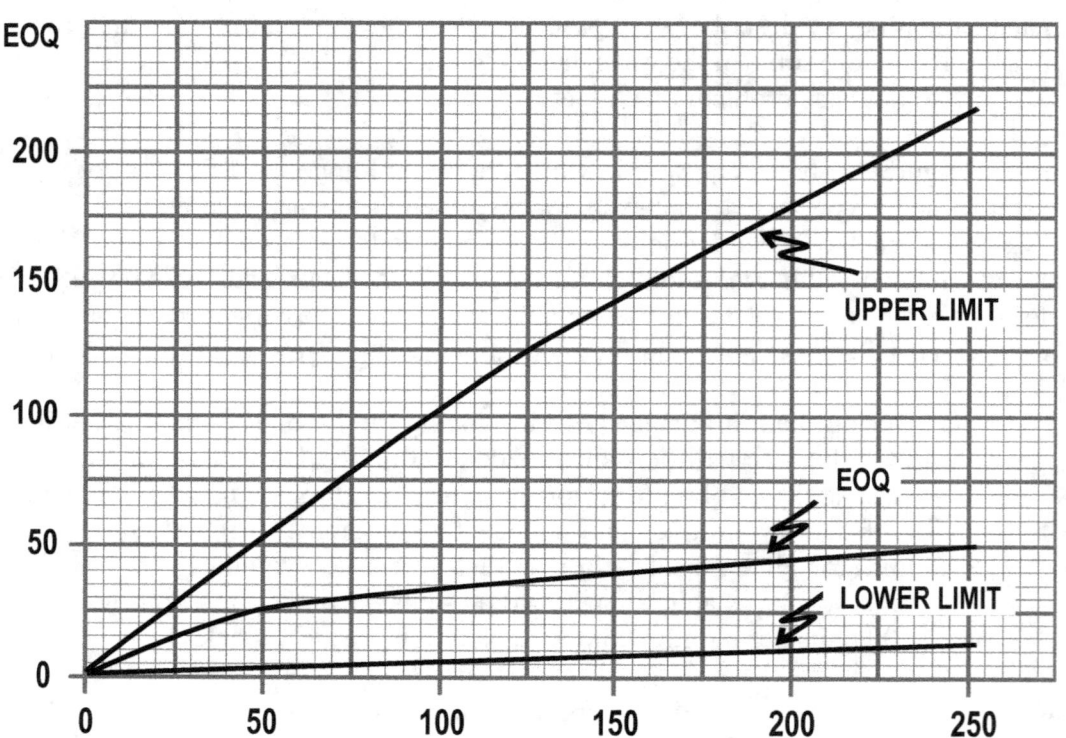

SALES OR USAGE (S)

FIGURE #6

CASE PROBLEM

ORDER POINT CURVE

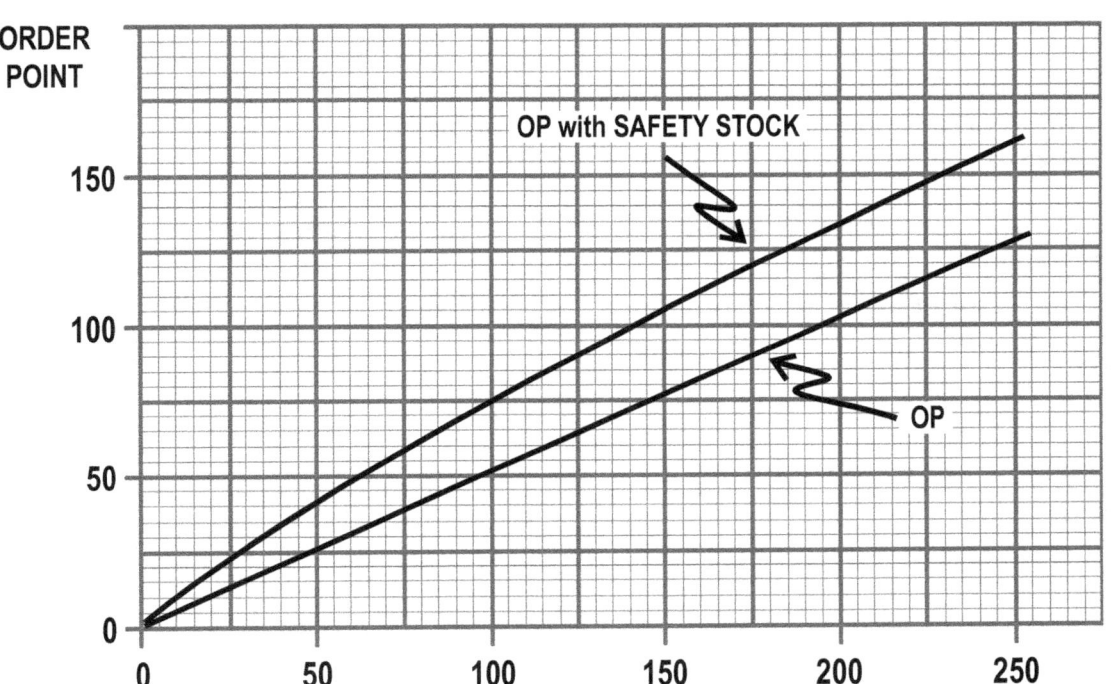

SALES OR USAGE (S)

The important conclusion to draw from the above discussion is that management by reference to charts or graphs of this type could establish some simple rules which would effectively control the production of this product.

CONCLUSION

Interpretation of the EOQ as a quantity range rather than a specific quantity is an important concept to understand in the formulation of your inventory control program. It will provide the line organization responsible for the day-to-day management of your inventories with the flexibility they must have to meet the demands placed on the system by daily production and sales problems.

A knowledge of algebra is all that is required to understand the EOQ Range formula as derived for you in Appendix D. At the conclusion of this Appendix, a simplified procedure is provided for applying the formula and calculating specific EOQ Ranges.

To assist you in evaluating how the EOQ Range concept might affect your inventory program, we have provided in Appendix E a series of EOQ Range tables for various combinations of values for the variables upon which the formula is based.

Chapter IV

Purchase Quantity

Occasionally you will hear a Purchasing Agent or Distributor ask the question, "The EOQ formula is fine for advising the manufacturer how much to make, but can we use it to determine how much to buy?" The answer to this question is a very definite, "Yes."

$$EOQ = \sqrt{\frac{2SO}{RU}}$$

S = Sales or Usage   O = Ordering Costs
R = Investment Factor   U = Unit Costs

The EOQ formula shown above is applicable to both manufacturing and purchasing situations. Appendix A provides a thorough analysis of how each variable used in the EOQ equation is evaluated depending upon whether the item is manufactured or purchased. Appendix C includes a review of the modifications required in the derivation of the EOQ formula to adapt it to a purchased item.

QUANTITY DISCOUNT

A common practice in industry today is the quantity discount which is used to encourage buyers to place larger orders. Many suppliers offer a discount schedule wherein the discount increases with the number of units ordered. The result is a variable unit cost for the item which is dependent on the quantity ordered. This problem does not exist for the manufacturer as his unit cost (U), as defined and used in the EOQ formula, can usually be considered constant. This brings us to the question, "How is the Quantity Discount and the resulting variable unit cost recognized in determining the EOQ for purchased items?"

The procedure for handling a quantity discount in the EOQ formula is not difficult, particularly if we analyze the problem and break it down into its logical components. The effect of a quantity discount is to produce several unit costs for the same item. These unit costs are dependent on the order quantity which determines the applicable discount. For each unit cost, we can calculate an economic order quantity using the EOQ formula. The optimum order quantity will be the largest EOQ provided it falls within the quantity range upon which the unit cost and respective discount is based. Let us use an example to illustrate this.

A company has a monthly usage of 100 units of Item A which can be purchased according to the following discount schedule:

	Purchase Quantity	Discount	Net Purchase Price per Unit
a)	1-9	—	$10.00
b)	10-49	10%	9.00
c)	50-99	25%	7.50
d)	over 100	40%	6.00

Assume the company has an established procedure for determining purchase order quantities based on the use of the EOQ formula and the following data is applicable to Item A:

Investment Factor (R)	=	24% per year
Ordering Costs (O)	=	$1.20 per order
Unit Costs (U)	=	Net Purchase Price per unit *plus* 20% for inventory carrying costs, taxes, handling, insurance, inspection, etc.

Using the above data and sales (S) of 100 units per month, we can calculate the respective EOQs for the 4 unit costs provided by the discount schedule.

	(a)	(b)	(c)	(d)
Monthly Sales (S)	100	100	100	100
Investment Factor (R)	24%	24%	24%	24%
Ordering Costs (O)	$1.20	$1.20	$1.20	$1.20
Unit Costs (U)	$12.00	$10.80	$9.00	$7.20
EOQ	32	34	36	41
Purchase Quantity*	1-9	10-49	50-99	over 100

Note:
*Purchase quantity required to obtain Net Purchase Price per Unit upon which Unit Cost (U) is based.

As shown above, the 4 EOQs vary from 32 to 41. The optimum EOQ is 34 as it is the largest EOQ which falls within its respective purchase quantity range (10-49). Theoretically, the EOQ of 36 cannot be used as it is based on a unit cost of

$9.00 which can be realized only if the order quantity is for 50-99 units. For the same reason, the EOQ of 41 cannot be used as its unit cost of $7.20 requires an order quantity of 100 or more units.

CONCLUSION

The above procedure is shown for those who wish to apply an exact and rigorous method to the determination of an EOQ for purchased items, the net price for which is determined by a quantity discount schedule. Although the above example is based on a single set of conditions, it supports the conclusion that very little is gained by this detailed probing of the problem. All 4 of the EOQs which range from 32 to 41, are within the discount bracket established by a purchase quantity of 10 to 49 units. Based on an expanded series of similar examples, it can be shown that the typical quantity discount schedule has no significant effect on the EOQ. At best, recognition of a purchase quantity discount will increase the order quantity only to the next discount bracket.

An easy solution to this problem is to base the purchase order quantity on an evaluation of the EOQ Range for the item and the respective discount schedule. By reference to Appendix E, we can see that the EOQ Range for Item A is from 18 to 56 units based on a value of 0.1% for the EOQ Control Limit (T). In view of this, justification could be made for establishing an order quantity for Item A of 50 units which would make the order eligible for the next higher discount bracket of 25%.

Here then is another valuable use for the EOQ Range formula. By interpreting the order quantity as a range rather than a specific amount, judgment can be used in selecting and optimizing an available purchase quantity discount schedule.

Chapter V

Summary

The universal question we all seek an answer to is, "What is an optimum inventory level?" The problem of answering this question is compounded by the fact that within a management group there are usually several conflicting opinions. The Sales Manager will not tolerate stock-outs. The Factory Manager desires long manufacturing runs and stable employment. The Treasurer feels that a minimum of working capital should be tied up in inventories.

Many companies blame their inventory problems on a large volume of small orders for diversified products: "We inventory 100,000 items." "Our sales forecasts are too general." "We're really a job shop." Each company feels that their problems in this respect are unusual. Refuge, however, cannot (and should not) be taken behind this smoke-screen. These problems are shared by most manufacturers today. If it is not apparent in some companies, perhaps the answer lies in the fact that their management has been able to minimize the problem.

Mr. John F. Magee in his article, "Guides to Inventory Policy," published in the January-February 1956 issue of the "Harvard Business Review," ably summarizes the problems inherent in converting inventory policies and practices from an intuitive process to one involving a more systematic and scientific approach.

"The questions businessmen raise in connection with management and control of inventories are basically aimed at action, not at arriving at answers. The questions are stated, unsurprisingly, in the characteristic terms of decisions to be made: 'Where shall we maintain how much stock?' 'Who will be responsible for it?' 'What shall we do to control balances or set proper schedules?' A manager necessarily thinks of problems in production planning in terms of centers of responsibility.

"However, action questions are not enough by themselves. In order to get at the answers to these questions as a basis for taking action, it is necessary to back off and ask some rather different kinds of questions: 'Why do we have inventories?' 'What affects the inventory balances we maintain?' 'How do these effects take place?' From these questions, a picture of the inventory problem can be built up which shows the influence on inventories and costs of the various alternative decisions which the management may ultimately want to consider.

"This type of analytic or functional question has been answered intuitively by businessmen with considerable success in the past. Consequently, most of the effort toward improved inventory management has been spent in other directions;

it has been aimed at better means for recording, filing, or displaying information and at better ways of doing the necessary clerical work. This is all to the good, for efficient data-handling helps. However, it does not lessen the need for a more systematic approach to inventory problems that can take the place of, or at least supplement, intuition.

"As business has grown, it has become more complex, and as business executives have become more and more specialized in their jobs or farther removed from direct operations, the task of achieving an economical balance intuitively has become increasingly difficult. That is why more businessmen are finding the concepts and mathematics of the growing field of inventory theory to be of direct practical help.

"One of the principal difficulties in the intuitive approach is that the types and definitions of cost which influence appropriate inventory policy are not those characteristically found on the books of a company. Many costs such as setup or purchasing costs are hidden in the accounting records. Others such as inventory capital costs may never appear at all. Each cost may be clear to the operating head primarily responsible for its control; since it is a 'hidden' cost, however, its importance may not be clear at all to other operating executives concerned. The resulting confusion may make it difficult to arrive at anything like a consistent policy."

The key to good inventory control primarily rests in sufficient knowledge of the fundamental techniques to develop enough self-confidence to permit their practical adaptation to the specific needs of the Company. Many programs are defeated before they start by imposing upon the group responsible for the execution of the program a "bag of tools" in the guise of mysterious mathematical equations and unique concepts. Seldom is any attempt made first to educate the group on how to use these new tools. The result is distrust of the techniques, poor application and eventually confusion when things get worse rather than better.

In establishing or improving upon inventory control procedures, it is important to remember the following fundamentals largely determine the degree of your success:

(1) The order point (OP) is singularly the most significant factor affecting your inventory control procedure as it establishes your inventory levels. Hence it determines your investment in inventories and your ability to provide satisfactory customer service. Careful attention must be given to the development of your order point procedure. Despite the several factors involved in the formula, remember it is primarily dependent on the accuracy of your sales or usage forecast.

(2) The EOQ is usually given far too much emphasis and often a disproportionate amount of time is spent worrying about unit costs, setup costs and the investment factor. Keep in mind these factors are not involved in determining your order point. The only factor common to both the OP and EOQ is the sales or usage variable. As already shown, the EOQ under most conditions can be interpreted as a broad quantity range.

It is perhaps appropriate to close this article with a reminder that regardless of how sophisticated your inventory control techniques, the results will be no better than the day-to-day data fed into the system. Before embarking on any elaborate inventory control program, be sure your accounting and record-keeping procedures can provide the system with current and reliable data. The bottleneck in most inventory control procedures is data input and utilization. It is in this area that we have seen many successful applications of Data Processing equipment.

A modern inventory control program affects all phases of your business, therefore, it must be an integral part of your business operation. The degree of success of an inventory program depends largely on how well management conceives the problem, formulates its policy and executes the program.

Chapter VI
Appendices

Definition of Variables

This schedule contains a discussion of the eight basic variables used in the Ordering Point (OP) and Economic Ordering Quantity (EOQ) equations. In relating specific data to these variables it is most important to recognize the dimension of these variables as discussed in the last section of this schedule.

S = Sales or Usage

This represents the forecast of future sales or usage. How far into the future the forecast is made is dependent primarily on the production or procurement cycle and the characteristics of the sales pattern. The usual practice is to make a forecast of from 3 to 6 months, normally through the projection of historical data. Sales forecasting is at best an inexact science, but every effort should be made to develop the very best possible projections.

P = Production or Procurement Cycle

This is the total elapsed time normally required to procure or manufacture the unit. In determining this time cycle, it should start when the decision is made that additional units are required and end with their delivery to the stock room or customer. If there are significant fluctuations in the time cycle, the effect on the Order Point should be tested for the probable extreme ranges of the cycle.

O = Ordering Costs

These are the variable costs associated with the manufacture or procurement of the lot size which are independent of the quantity. A typical list of these costs includes variable labor and expenses for: purchasing, receiving, accounting, planning and manufacturing setup.

U = Unit Costs

This includes the variable costs related to the production or procurement of each unit, such as the manufacturing cost or net purchase price per unit. To this must be added inventory carrying costs per unit for space, taxes, handling, insurance, inspection, etc.

K = Cost Ratio

K is the ratio of Ordering Costs (O) to Unit Costs (U) or $K = (O)/(U)$.

R = Investment Factor

The function of the investment factor is to provide a rate of return on the inventory investment (before taxes) which is commensurate with the risks and costs associated with the business, such as: obsolescence, cost of working capital, and spoiled work. In actual application, different interest rates can be used depending on the degree of risk involved. Factors which should be considered in evaluating the degree of risk are: type of product, reliability of the sales or usage forecast, working capital requirements, etc.

L = Lead Time

Lead time can be defined as the average time span between the acceptance of an order and the promised delivery date. For repair parts and critical stock items, the lead time is often zero, whereas for a large machine tool the lead time may vary from three to nine months. Lead time is primarily a function of the nature of the product and competitive practices.

Q = Units Per Demand

Units per demand refers to the average number of units per order. For instance, an automotive distributor will usually receive orders for spark plugs or valves in 6 or 8 units per demand.

F = Stockout Acceptance Factor

The significance of the Stockout Acceptance Factor (F) is discussed in the report under the section "Order Point." The value of F in the Order Point equation for a given per cent stockout level, assuming a Poisson Distribution in the demand pattern, can be read from the graph shown in Figure #7.

T = EOQ Control Limit

In Appendix D, an equation has been developed for the calculation of the EOQ Range. This function is based on an acceptable percentage increase in the minimum total variable unit cost. The percentage increase is termed the EOQ Control Limit and designated by the letter (T).

Dimension of the Variables

In the use of the Order Point (OP), Economic Order Quantity (EOQ), and EOQ Range equations, it is critical that all data be in the same time or units dimension, for example:

Variable	Value of Raw Data	Formula Value Per Month	Per Week
S	200 per month	200	46.2
P	6 weeks	1.39	6
L	1 month	1	4.33
R	24% per year	.02	.0046
O	50 cents per lot	.50	.50
U	$3.00 per unit	3.00	3.00
Q	5 per demand	5	5
F	2.06	2.06	2.06
T	½ of 1%	.005	.005

FIGURE #7

STOCK-OUT ACCEPTANCE FACTOR

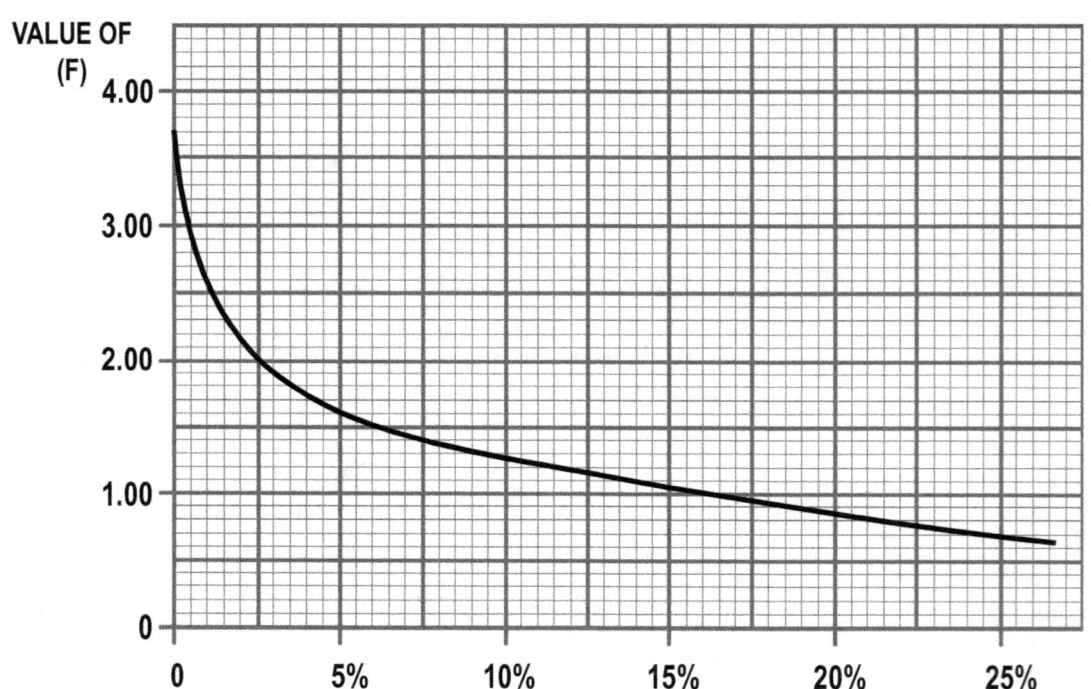

ACCEPTABLE STOCK-OUT PERCENTAGE

Derivation of The
Order Point (OP) Equation

The purpose of the Order Point (OP) is to signal when the level of a particular item in inventory has reached the point where, based on forecasted usage, it will be completely exhausted during the time required to manufacture or produce a replenishment stock. The variables used in the derivation of the equation are:

S = Sales or Usage
L = Lead Time
Q = Units Per Demand
F = Stockout Acceptance Factor
P = Production or Procurement Cycle

The equation can be derived as follows:

1) Assuming uniform usage by single units and no lead time or safety stock:

$$(OP) = S \times P$$

2) Allowing for a lead time L:

$$(OP) = S(P\text{-}L)$$

3) Providing for a safety stock based on a demand pattern similar to the Poisson Distribution:

$$(OP) = S(P\text{-}L) + F\sqrt{S(P-L)}$$

4) Recognizing a usage which has an average of (Q) items per demand:

$$(OP) - Q\left[\frac{S}{Q}(P-L) + F\sqrt{\frac{S}{Q}(P-L)}\ \right]$$

$$= S(P\text{-}L) + F\sqrt{SQ(P-L)}$$

Appendix C

Derivation of The
Economic Ordering Quantity
(EOQ Formula)

As previously emphasized, to effectively use and apply the EOQ formula, those persons responsible for the formulation of the inventory control program should be familiar with its derivation and, in particular, the assumptions it is based upon. Figure #8 shows the familiar configuration of curves associated with the EOQ equation. These curves are plotted to scale using the data for the case problem discussed in Chapter III.

Curve I represents the variable cost per unit to manufacture or produce an ordering quantity of (N). As expected, the manufacturing or procurement costs per unit reduce as the ordering quantity increases, eventually becoming asymptotic to the x-axis at a value equal to the unit cost (U). Curve II is the variable inventory carrying costs per unit. Curve III is the sum of Curves I and II, and, therefore, is the total cost per unit as a function of the lot size (N). The economic ordering quantity is that number of units which will produce the minimum cost per unit and is shown as the point (EOQ).

The following variables are involved in the derivation of the (EOQ) formula:

S = Sales or Usage
R = Investment Factor
O = Ordering Costs
U = Unit Costs
P = Production or Procurement Cycle

The derivation of the EOQ formula is as follows:

1) The equation for Curve I, the cost to manufacture or procure a unit for a given ordering quantity (N), is:

$$\text{Let } (x) = \frac{O}{N} + U$$

2) For manufactured parts, it is assumed that the work-in-process inventory value accumulates in a constant and uniform manner during the production cycle to a total value of (Nx). The average value of the

FIGURE #8

UNIT COST CURVES

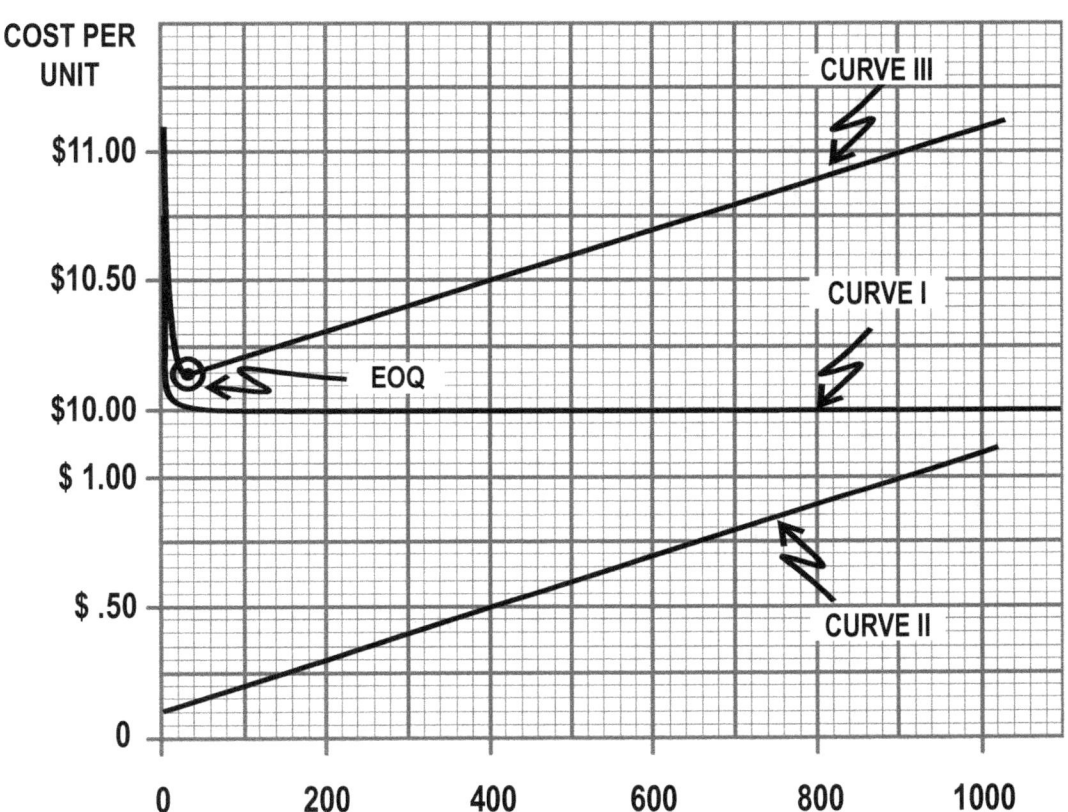

QUANTITY ORDERED (N)

inventory investment during the production cycle is, therefore, equal to one-half of the total inventory value or ($\frac{1}{2}$ Nx). The inventory carrying costs for an ordering quantity (N) during the production cycle (P) can be expressed as the product of the following variables:

$$\text{Let (y)} = \frac{NRPx}{2}$$

Obviously, this step does not apply to items purchased direct for finished inventory stock and are not involved in the manufacturing cycle.

3) The manufactured or purchased lot size has a finished inventory value equal to (Nx). Assuming one immediate sale and the depletion of the remaining stock in a constant and uniform manner during the sales or usage cycle, the inventory carrying costs during this cycle can be expressed as follows:

$$\text{Let (z)} = \left[\frac{NRx}{2}\right]\left[\frac{N-1}{S}\right]$$

4) The equation for Curve II, the inventory carrying costs per unit incurred during the production and sales cycle, is the sum of functions (y) and (z) or:

$$\text{Let (w)} = \frac{(y)+(z)}{N}$$

5) Curve III represents the total cost per unit (TUC) to manufacture (x) and carry in inventory (w) a given lot size (N). This can be expressed as:

$$\text{TUC} = (x)+(w) = \left[\frac{O}{N}+U\right]\left[1+\frac{RP}{2}+\frac{RN}{2S}+\frac{R}{2S}\right]$$

6) The economic ordering quantity or the EOQ point can be found by differentiating the total unit cost equation (TUC) with respect to (N) and solving for the value of N with the derivative equal to zero, as shown in Step 8. The result is the equation:

$$\text{EOQ} = \sqrt{\frac{2SO}{RU}+\frac{PSO}{U}-\frac{O}{U}} = \sqrt{\frac{2SO}{RU}}$$

7) As previously stated in Step (1), the EOQ equation can be modified for purchased items by letting the value of (y) equal zero. When this is done, the result is simply the elimination of the middle term and the expression reduces to:

$$\text{EOQ} = \sqrt{\frac{2SO}{RU}-\frac{O}{U}} \cong \sqrt{\frac{2SO}{RU}}$$

8) The derivation of the EOQ equation from the algebraic expression for the total cost equation (TUC) is as follows:

a) Let $A = 1 + \dfrac{RP}{2} - \dfrac{R}{2S}$ and $B = \dfrac{R}{2S}$

b) Then

$$TUC = \left[\frac{O}{N} + U\right][A + BN] = \frac{OA}{N} + OB + UA + UBN$$

c) To minimize, take the first derivative with respect to N, set it equal to zero and solve for N.

$$\frac{d(TUC)}{dN} = -OA + UBN^2$$

$$N = \sqrt{\frac{OA}{UB}} = \sqrt{\frac{2SO}{RU} + \frac{PSO}{U} - \frac{O}{U}}$$

Derivation of The
EOQ Range Formula

The theory and general discussion concerning the development and application of the EOQ Range Formula is provided in Chapter III. The purpose of this schedule is to present the derivation of the equation.

DERIVATION

1) The minimum total unit cost is obtained when the EOQ lot size (No) is used. Using the expression developed in Section 8b of Appendix C, this can be expressed as follows:

$$\text{Minimum Unit Cost} = \text{Co} = \left[\frac{O}{No} + U\right] \left[A + BNo\right]$$

2) A change in the lot size (n) will result in an increase in the unit cost (c).

$$\text{New Cost} = \text{Co} + c = \left[\frac{O}{No + n} + U\right] \left[A + BNo + Bn\right]$$

3) The expression for the change in cost (c) can be derived by subtracting the New Cost (2) from the Minimum Unit Cost (1):

$$(2) - (1) = c = \left[\frac{AO}{No}\right] \left[\frac{X^2}{1+X}\right] \text{ where } X = \left[\frac{n}{No}\right]$$

4) The proportional increase in unit cost (T) can be defined as:

$$T = \frac{c}{Co} = \left[\frac{AO}{CoNo}\right] \left[\frac{X^2}{1+X}\right]$$

5) Substituting in the general expressions for Co and No as derived in the preceding sections:

$$T = \frac{YX^2}{(1+Y)^2(1+X)} \text{ where } Y = \sqrt{\frac{BO}{AU}}$$

6) The function for (T) can be simplified and expressed as a quadratic equation:

$$T(1+Y)^2 \ (1+X) = YX^2$$

$$\frac{X^2}{(1+X)} = \frac{T(1+Y)^2}{Y} = M$$

$$X^2 = M(1+X)$$

$$X^2 = MX - M = 0$$

7) The values for X can be obtained by using the general solution for a quadratic equation:

$$X, \text{ and } X_2 = \frac{M \pm \sqrt{M^2 + 4M}}{2}$$

8) The EOQ Range Formula, where No = EOQ, is:

$$N_1 \text{ --- No } (1+X_1)$$

$$N_2 \text{ --- No } (1+X_2)$$

PROCEDURE FOR CALCULATING EOQ RANGE

The procedure for calculating the EOQ Range represented by N and N2 for a given derivation (T) from the minimum unit cost (Co) is:

a) Calculate the values for the following:

$$A = 1 + \frac{RP}{2} - \frac{R}{2S}$$

$$B = \frac{R}{2S}$$

$$K = \frac{O}{U}$$

b) Determine the value of the following expressions:

$$Y = \sqrt{\frac{BK}{A}}$$

$$M = \frac{T(1+Y)^2}{Y}$$

c) Solve for the values of X_1 and X_2:

$$X_1 = \frac{M + \sqrt{M^2 + 4M}}{2}$$

$$X_2 = \frac{M - \sqrt{M^2 + 4M}}{2}$$

d) Calculate the EOQ Range:

$$EOQ = No = \sqrt{\frac{AK}{B}}$$

$$N_1 = No\ (X_1+1)$$

$$N_2 = No\ (X_2+1)$$

EOQ Range Tables

P = Production or Procurement Cycle

Example: .50 = ½ month

Tables for production or procurement cycles of 0.5 and 6 months are provided to show that this variable has very little effect on the EOQ. As discussed in Chapter II, the production or procurement cycle is not a significant factor in determining the EOQ and is, therefore, eliminated in the simplified expression of the formula.

K = Cost Ratio

Example: K is the ratio of Ordering Costs (O) to Unit Costs (U) or (O)/(U). Therefore if K = 0.10, the Unit Cost is ten times greater than the Ordering Cost.

R = Investment Factor

Example: .02 = 2% per month or 24% per year

S = Sales or Usage

Example: 10 = sale or usage of 10 units per month

T = EOQ Control Limit

Example: T = .1%, the EOQ Range is based on an acceptable increase in the minimum total variable unit cost of 1/10 of 1%.

Example (See Page 51)

P = .50		EOQ = 32
K = .10		EOQ Range (T = 0.1%) = 18 – 56
R = .01		EOQ Range (T = 0.5%) = 10 – 105
S = 50		

Value of Variables (Monthly Base)			EOQ AND EOQ RANGE BY PERCENTAGE INCREASE (T) IN TOTAL COST					
P	K	R	S	.5%	.1%	EOQ	.1%	.5%
.50	.01	.0050	1	1	1	2	3	5
			5	1	2	4	8	16
			10	1	3	6	13	30
			20	1	4	9	22	57
			30	1	4	11	30	81
			50	2	5	14	43	126
			75	2	5	17	59	180
			100	2	5	20	75	239
			250	2	6	32	159	569
			500	2	7	45	284	1095
			750	2	7	55	404	1616
			1000	2	8	63	517	2118
.50	.01	.0100	1		1	1	1	2
			5	1	2	3	5	10
			10	1	2	4	8	16
			20	1	3	6	13	30
			30	1	3	8	19	46
			50	1	4	10	26	69
			75	1	4	12	35	96
			100	2	5	14	43	126
			250	2	6	22	88	289
			500	2	6	32	159	569
			750	2	7	39	222	833
			1000	2	7	45	284	1096
.50	.01	.0200	1		1	1	1	2
			5	1	1	2	3	6
			10	1	2	3	5	10
			20	1	2	4	8	16
			30	1	2	5	10	23
			50	1	3	7	16	38
			75	1	4	9	22	56
			100	1	4	10	26	69
			250	2	5	16	53	157
			500	2	6	22	88	289
			750	2	6	27	122	423
			1000	2	6	32	159	570
.50	.01	.0300	1	1	1	1	1	2
			5	1	1	2	3	5
			10	1	2	3	5	9
			20	1	2	4	7	14
			30	1	2	4	8	16
			50	1	3	6	13	28
			75	1	3	7	16	38
			100	2	3	8	19	48
			250	2	4	13	38	109
			500	2	5	18	64	199
			750	2	6	22	88	289
			1000	2	6	26	113	387

Value of Variables (Monthly Base)			EOQ AND EOQ RANGE BY PERCENTAGE INCREASE (T) IN TOTAL COST					
P	K	R	S	.5%	.1%	EOQ	.1%	.5%
.50	.01	.0050	1	3	5	6	8	11
			5	6	10	14	20	32
			10	8	13	20	31	53
			20	9	17	28	47	87
			30	10	20	35	63	121
			50	11	23	45	87	180
			75	12	27	55	114	249
			100	13	29	63	137	313
			250	15	38	100	262	687
			500	16	46	142	439	1274
			750	16	50	173	596	1831
			1000	17	54	200	747	2386
.50	.01	.0100	1	2	3	4	5	6
			5	5	7	10	14	20
			10	6	10	14	20	32
			20	8	13	20	31	53
			30	9	15	25	41	72
			50	10	18	32	56	105
			75	11	21	39	72	143
			100	11	23	45	87	180
			250	13	31	71	161	381
			500	15	38	100	262	687
			750	15	43	123	354	986
			1000	16	46	142	439	1275
.50	.01	.0200	1	2	2	3	4	5
			5	4	5	7	9	13
			10	5	7	10	14	20
			20	6	10	14	20	32
			30	7	11	17	26	42
			50	8	14	22	35	61
			75	9	16	27	45	82
			100	10	18	32	56	105
			250	12	25	50	100	214
			500	13	31	71	161	381
			750	14	35	87	214	538
			1000	15	38	100	262	688
.50	.01	.0300	1	2	3	3	4	4
			5	3	5	6	8	10
			10	4	6	8	11	15
			20	6	9	12	17	25
			30	6	10	14	20	32
			50	7	12	18	28	46
			75	8	14	22	35	61
			100	9	16	26	43	77
			250	11	22	41	77	156
			500	12	28	58	122	272
			750	13	31	71	161	381
			1000	14	34	82	197	487

Value of Variables (Monthly Base)			EOQ AND EOQ RANGE BY PERCENTAGE INCREASE (T) IN TOTAL COST					
P	K	R	S	.5%	.1%	EOQ	.1%	.5%
.50	.01	.0050	1	14	17	20	23	28
			5	28	36	45	56	73
			10	36	49	63	81	111
			20	46	66	89	120	173
			30	53	79	110	153	228
			50	62	97	142	207	324
			75	70	114	173	262	428
			100	76	128	200	312	526
			250	96	181	316	552	1039
			500	112	231	447	864	1787
			750	121	265	548	1132	2482
			1000	127	291	633	1377	3148
.50	.01	.0100	1	11	12	14	16	19
			5	21	27	32	38	48
			10	28	36	45	56	73
			20	36	49	63	81	111
			30	42	59	78	103	145
			50	50	73	100	137	201
			75	57	87	123	175	266
			100	62	97	142	207	324
			250	81	140	224	359	620
			500	96	182	317	553	1043
			750	106	210	388	717	1427
			1000	112	232	448	866	1791
.50	.01	.0200	1	1	4	10	26	69
			5	16	19	22	26	31
			10	21	27	32	38	48
			20	28	36	45	56	73
			30	32	43	55	70	93
			50	39	54	71	93	129
			75	45	65	87	117	167
			100	50	73	100	137	201
			250	67	107	159	237	379
			500	81	140	224	359	620
			750	90	163	275	463	840
			1000	96	182	137	554	1043
.50	.01	.0300	1	1	3	8	19	47
			5	13	16	18	21	25
			10	18	22	26	31	38
			20	24	30	37	45	57
			30	28	36	45	56	73
			50	34	45	58	74	100
			75	39	54	71	93	129
			100	43	61	82	109	155
			250	59	91	130	186	287
			500	72	119	183	281	463
			750	81	140	224	359	621
			1000	87	156	259	429	769

Value of Variables (Monthly Base)			EOQ AND EOQ RANGE BY PERCENTAGE INCREASE (T) IN TOTAL COST					
P	K	R	S	.5%	.1%	EOQ	.1%	.5%
.50	2.00	.0050	1	21	25	28	32	37
			5	42	52	63	76	95
			10	55	72	89	110	144
			20	72	98	127	164	223
			30	83	117	155	205	288
			50	99	146	200	275	403
			75	113	172	245	348	529
			100	124	194	283	412	645
			250	162	279	447	716	1237
			500	192	363	633	1105	2081
			750	211	419	775	1433	2849
			1000	224	463	895	1729	3578
.50	2.00	.0100	1	3	8	20	52	137
			5	32	38	45	53	64
			10	42	52	63	76	95
			20	56	73	90	112	145
			30	65	87	110	140	183
			50	78	109	142	186	257
			75	90	129	173	233	333
			100	99	146	200	275	403
			250	133	213	317	472	755
			500	162	280	448	717	1240
			750	179	326	548	921	1673
			1000	192	363	633	1105	2082
.50	2.00	.0200	1	3	6	14	32	75
			5	24	28	32	37	43
			10	32	38	45	53	64
			20	42	52	63	76	95
			30	50	64	78	95	122
			50	60	80	100	126	166
			75	71	96	123	158	214
			100	78	109	142	186	257
			250	107	160	224	313	469
			500	133	213	317	472	755
			750	149	250	388	602	1007
			1000	162	280	448	718	1241
.50	2.00	.0300	1	3	6	12	25	56
			5	20	23	26	29	34
			10	27	32	37	43	51
			20	36	44	52	61	75
			30	42	52	63	76	95
			50	52	67	82	101	130
			75	60	80	100	126	166
			100	68	91	116	148	199
			250	94	135	183	248	358
			500	118	181	259	371	571
			750	133	213	317	472	756
			1000	145	239	367	563	929

Value of Variables (Monthly Base)			EOQ AND EOQ RANGE BY PERCENTAGE INCREASE (T) IN TOTAL COST					
P	K	R	S	.5%	.1%	EOQ	.1%	.5%
3.00	.01	.0050	1	1	1	2	3	5
			5	1	2	4	8	16
			10	1	3	6	13	30
			20	1	4	9	22	57
			30	1	4	11	30	81
			50	2	5	14	43	126
			75	2	5	17	59	180
			100	2	5	20	75	239
			250	2	6	32	159	570
			500	2	7	45	285	1099
			750	2	7	55	405	1621
			1000	2	8	63	518	2124
3.00	.01	.0100	1		1	1	1	2
			5	1	2	3	5	10
			10	1	3	5	10	20
			20	1	3	6	13	30
			30	1	3	8	19	46
			50	1	4	10	26	69
			75	1	4	12	35	97
			100	2	5	14	43	126
			250	2	6	23	92	304
			500	2	6	32	160	572
			750	2	7	39	223	837
			1000	2	7	45	286	1102
3.00	.01	.0200	1		1	1	1	2
			5	1	1	2	3	6
			10	1	2	3	5	10
			20	1	3	5	10	20
			30	1	3	6	12	27
			50	1	3	7	16	38
			75	1	4	9	22	56
			100	1	4	10	26	69
			250	2	5	16	53	159
			500	2	6	23	93	305
			750	2	6	28	128	444
			1000	2	6	32	160	576
3.00	.01	.0300	1	1	1	1	1	2
			5	1	1	2	3	5
			10	1	2	3	5	9
			20	1	2	4	7	14
			30	1	3	5	10	20
			50	1	3	6	13	29
			75	1	3	7	16	38
			100	1	3	8	19	48
			250	2	4	13	39	110
			500	2	5	19	68	214
			750	2	6	23	93	307
			1000	2	6	26	115	394

Value of Variables (Monthly Base)			EOQ AND EOQ RANGE BY PERCENTAGE INCREASE (T) IN TOTAL COST					
P	K	R	S	.5%	.1%	EOQ	.1%	.5%
3.00	.10	.0050	1	3	5	6	8	11
			5	6	10	14	20	32
			10	8	13	20	31	53
			20	9	17	28	47	87
			30	10	20	35	63	121
			50	11	23	45	87	180
			75	12	27	55	114	250
			100	13	29	63	137	314
			250	15	38	100	262	688
			500	16	46	142	440	1277
			750	16	50	174	600	1846
			1000	17	54	201	752	2405
3.00	.10	.0100	1	2	3	4	5	6
			5	5	7	10	14	20
			10	6	10	14	20	32
			20	8	13	20	31	53
			30	9	15	25	41	72
			50	10	18	32	56	106
			75	11	21	39	72	144
			100	11	23	45	87	181
			250	13	31	71	162	382
			500	15	38	101	266	697
			750	15	43	123	355	991
			1000	16	46	142	441	1281
3.00	.10	.0200	1	2	2	3	4	5
			5	4	5	7	9	13
			10	5	7	10	14	20
			20	6	10	14	20	32
			30	7	12	18	27	45
			50	8	14	23	37	64
			75	9	17	28	47	86
			100	10	18	32	56	106
			250	12	25	51	103	220
			500	13	32	72	164	390
			750	14	36	88	218	550
			1000	15	38	101	266	701
3.00	.10	.0300	1	2	3	3	4	4
			5	3	5	6	8	10
			10	4	6	8	11	15
			20	6	9	12	17	26
			30	6	10	14	20	32
			50	7	12	19	29	48
			75	8	14	23	37	64
			100	9	16	26	43	78
			250	11	22	42	79	161
			500	12	28	59	125	280
			750	13	31	72	165	392
			1000	14	34	83	201	499

Value of Variables (Monthly Base)			EOQ AND EOQ RANGE BY PERCENTAGE INCREASE (T) IN TOTAL COST					
P	K	R	S	.5%	.1%	EOQ	.1%	.5%
3.00	1.00	.0050	1	14	17	20	23	28
			5	28	36	45	56	73
			10	36	49	63	81	111
			20	46	67	90	122	175
			30	53	79	110	153	229
			50	62	97	142	207	324
			75	70	115	174	264	431
			100	76	129	201	314	529
			250	96	181	317	554	1044
			500	112	232	449	868	1798
			750	121	266	550	1138	2496
			1000	127	292	635	1383	3165
3.00	1.00	.0100	1	11	12	14	16	19
			5	21	27	32	38	48
			10	28	36	45	56	73
			20	36	50	64	83	113
			30	42	59	78	103	145
			50	50	73	101	139	204
			75	57	86	123	175	266
			100	62	97	142	207	324
			250	81	140	225	361	625
			500	97	182	319	558	1053
			750	106	211	390	722	1439
			1000	112	233	451	873	1810
3.00	1.00	.0200	1	8	9	10	11	13
			5	16	20	23	27	33
			10	21	27	32	38	48
			20	28	36	45	56	73
			30	33	44	56	71	95
			50	40	55	72	94	131
			75	46	65	88	119	170
			100	50	73	101	139	204
			250	67	107	160	239	383
			500	81	141	227	365	632
			750	90	165	278	469	855
			1000	97	183	321	562	1063
3.00	1.00	.0300	1	1	3	8	19	48
			5	14	16	19	22	26
			10	18	22	26	31	38
			20	24	30	37	45	57
			30	28	37	46	57	75
			50	34	46	59	75	102
			75	39	55	72	94	131
			100	44	62	83	111	158
			250	59	92	132	190	293
			500	73	122	187	288	477
			750	82	142	229	368	640
			1000	88	159	264	440	791

Value of Variables (Monthly Base)			EOQ AND EOQ RANGE BY PERCENTAGE INCREASE (T) IN TOTAL COST					
P	K	R	S	.5%	.1%	EOQ	.1%	.5%
3.00	2.00	.0050	1	21	25	28	32	37
			5	42	52	63	76	95
			10	56	73	90	112	145
			20	72	98	127	164	223
			30	83	117	155	205	289
			50	100	146	201	276	405
			75	114	173	246	350	532
			100	124	195	284	414	648
			250	162	280	449	719	1244
			500	193	363	635	1109	2091
			750	211	420	777	1438	2861
			1000	224	464	898	1736	3596
3.00	2.00	.0100	1	16	18	20	22	26
			5	32	38	45	53	64
			10	43	53	64	77	96
			20	56	73	90	112	145
			30	65	87	110	140	187
			50	78	108	142	186	258
			75	90	129	174	234	335
			100	100	146	201	277	406
			250	134	214	319	475	762
			500	162	281	451	723	1252
			750	180	328	552	930	1691
			1000	193	364	637	1114	2102
3.00	2.00	.0200	1	3	6	14	32	76
			5	24	28	32	37	43
			10	32	38	45	53	64
			20	42	53	64	77	96
			30	50	65	79	97	124
			50	61	80	101	127	168
			75	71	96	124	160	217
			100	79	110	144	189	262
			250	108	162	227	318	477
			500	134	215	321	479	769
			750	151	253	393	611	1025
			1000	163	283	454	729	1265
3.00	2.00	.0300	1	3	6	12	25	57
			5	20	23	26	29	34
			10	27	32	37	43	51
			20	36	45	53	63	77
			30	43	54	65	78	98
			50	52	67	83	102	132
			75	61	81	102	128	170
			100	68	92	118	151	204
			250	95	138	187	254	368
			500	119	183	264	380	586
			750	134	216	323	483	776
			1000	146	242	373	574	952

Reorder Point Table

P = Production or Procurement Cycle

Example: 1.00 = 1 month

L = Lead Time

Example: 1.00 = 1 month

Q = Units per Demand

Example: 10 = average order is for 10 units

S = Sales or Usage

Example: 10 = sale or usage of 10 units per month

Example (See Page 61)

P = 1.00	Reorder Point – 0% —	Stockout = 139
L = 0	Reorder Point – 5% —	Stockout = 87
Q = 10	Reorder Point – 10% —	Stockout = 79
S = 50	Reorder Point – 20% —	Stockout = 69

Value of Variables (Monthly Base)			REORDER POINT BY ALLOWED STOCK OUT PERCENTAGE				
P	L	Q	S	20%	10%	5%	0%
.50	0	1	1	1	1	2	3
			5	4	5	5	9
			10	7	8	9	14
			20	13	14	15	23
			30	18	20	21	30
			50	29	31	33	45
			75	43	45	48	62
			100	56	59	62	78
			250	135	139	144	170
			500	263	270	276	313
			750	391	400	407	452
			1000	519	529	537	589
.50	0	10	1	2	3	4	9
			5	7	9	11	23
			10	11	14	17	33
			20	19	23	27	50
			30	25	31	35	64
			50	38	45	51	88
			75	54	62	70	115
			100	69	79	87	139
			250	155	171	184	266
			500	293	315	334	450
			750	427	454	477	620
			1000	560	591	618	783
.50	0	50	1	5	7	9	21
			5	12	17	21	47
			10	18	25	31	68
			20	29	39	47	99
			30	38	50	61	125
			50	55	71	84	166
			75	74	93	110	211
			100	93	115	134	250
			250	192	227	257	441
			500	345	394	437	697
			750	491	552	604	923
			1000	634	704	764	1132
.50	0	100	1	7	10	12	29
			5	16	23	29	66
			10	24	34	42	94
			20	37	51	63	136
			30	48	65	80	170
			50	68	90	109	225
			75	90	117	140	282
			100	110	141	168	333
			250	220	269	312	572
			500	384	454	514	882
			750	540	625	689	1150
			1000	690	788	873	1394

Value of Variables (Monthly Base)			REORDER POINT BY ALLOWED STOCK OUT PERCENTAGE				
P	L	Q	S	20%	10%	5%	0%
1.00	0	1	1	2	2	3	5
			5	7	8	9	14
			10	13	14	15	23
			20	24	26	27	38
			30	35	37	39	52
			50	56	59	62	78
			75	82	86	89	110
			100	109	113	117	140
			250	263	270	276	313
			500	519	529	537	589
			750	773	785	796	860
			1000	1027	1041	1053	1126
1.00	0	10	1	4	5	6	14
			5	11	14	17	33
			10	19	23	27	50
			20	32	38	44	77
			30	45	52	59	99
			50	69	79	87	139
			75	98	110	121	185
			100	127	141	153	226
			250	293	315	334	450
			500	560	591	618	783
			750	824	862	895	1096
			1000	1085	1129	1167	1400
1.00	0	50	1	7	10	13	29
			5	18	25	31	68
			10	29	39	47	99
			20	47	61	73	146
			30	63	80	95	185
			50	93	115	134	250
			75	127	154	177	320
			100	160	191	218	383
			250	345	394	437	697
			500	634	704	764	1132
			750	915	1000	1073	1525
			1000	1190	1288	1373	1894
1.00	0	100	1	10	14	18	41
			5	24	34	42	94
			10	37	51	63	136
			20	58	78	95	199
			30	77	101	121	249
			50	110	141	168	333
			75	149	187	220	421
			100	185	229	267	500
			250	384	454	514	882
			500	690	788	873	1394
			750	983	1103	1207	1845
			1000	1269	1408	1528	2265

Value of Variables (Monthly Base)			REORDER POINT BY ALLOWED STOCK OUT PERCENTAGE				
P	L	Q	S	20%	10%	5%	0%
1.00	.50	1	1	1	1	2	3
			5	4	5	5	9
			10	7	8	9	14
			20	13	14	15	23
			30	18	20	21	30
			50	29	31	33	45
			75	43	45	48	62
			100	56	59	62	78
			250	135	139	144	170
			500	263	270	276	313
			750	391	400	407	452
			1000	519	529	537	589
1.00	.50	10	1	2	3	4	9
			5	7	9	11	23
			10	11	14	17	33
			20	19	23	27	50
			30	25	31	35	64
			50	38	45	51	88
			75	54	62	70	115
			100	69	79	87	139
			250	155	171	184	266
			500	293	315	334	450
			750	427	454	477	620
			1000	560	591	618	783
1.00	.50	50	1	5	7	9	21
			5	12	17	21	47
			10	18	25	31	68
			20	29	39	47	99
			30	38	50	61	125
			50	55	71	84	166
			75	74	93	110	211
			100	93	115	134	250
			250	192	227	257	441
			500	345	394	437	697
			750	491	552	604	923
			1000	634	704	764	1132
1.00	.50	100	1	7	10	12	29
			5	16	23	29	66
			10	24	34	42	94
			20	37	51	63	136
			30	48	65	80	170
			50	68	90	109	225
			75	90	117	140	282
			100	110	141	168	333
			250	220	269	312	572
			500	384	454	514	882
			750	540	625	698	1150
			1000	690	788	873	1394

Value of Variables (Monthly Base)			REORDER POINT BY ALLOWED STOCK OUT PERCENTAGE				
P	L	Q	S	20%	10%	5%	0%
3.00	0	1	1	4	5	6	10
			5	18	20	21	30
			10	35	37	39	52
			20	67	70	73	91
			30	98	102	106	128
			50	160	166	170	199
			75	238	244	250	285
			100	315	322	329	369
			250	773	785	796	860
			500	1533	1550	1565	1655
			750	2290	2311	2329	2440
			1000	3047	3071	3091	3219
3.00	0	10	1	8	10	12	25
			5	25	31	35	64
			10	45	52	59	99
			20	81	92	101	158
			30	116	129	140	210
			50	183	200	215	305
			75	265	286	304	415
			100	347	371	391	519
			250	824	862	895	1096
			500	1604	1658	1705	1990
			750	2378	2444	2501	2850
			1000	3147	3223	3289	3693
3.00	0	50	1	13	19	23	52
			5	38	50	61	125
			10	63	80	95	185
			20	107	131	151	279
			30	147	177	202	358
			50	224	262	295	496
			75	315	362	402	649
			100	404	458	505	790
			250	915	1000	1073	1525
			500	1733	1853	1957	2595
			750	2535	2683	2810	3592
			1000	3329	3500	3647	4549
3.00	0	100	1	18	25	32	72
			5	48	65	80	170
			10	77	101	121	249
			20	126	160	189	370
			30	171	212	248	469
			50	254	308	355	640
			75	353	419	476	825
			100	447	523	589	993
			250	983	1103	1207	1845
			500	1829	2000	2147	3049
			750	2653	2862	3042	4147
			1000	3466	3707	3915	5191

Value of Variables (Monthly Base)				REORDER POINT BY ALLOWED STOCK OUT PERCENTAGE			
P	L	Q	S	20%	10%	5%	0%
3.00	.50	1	1	4	5	5	9
			5	16	17	18	27
			10	29	31	33	45
			20	56	59	62	78
			30	82	86	89	110
			50	135	139	144	170
			75	199	205	210	242
			100	263	270	276	313
			250	646	657	667	725
			500	1280	1296	1309	1391
			750	1912	1931	1947	2048
			1000	2543	2565	2584	2700
3.00	.50	10	1	7	9	11	23
			5	22	27	31	57
			10	38	45	51	88
			20	69	79	87	139
			30	98	110	121	185
			50	155	171	184	266
			75	224	243	260	361
			100	293	315	334	450
			250	692	727	757	941
			500	1345	1394	1437	1697
			750	1991	2052	2104	2423
			1000	2634	2704	2764	3132
3.00	.50	50	1	12	17	21	47
			5	34	45	54	113
			10	55	71	84	166
			20	93	115	134	250
			30	127	154	177	320
			50	192	227	257	441
			75	270	312	349	575
			100	345	394	437	697
			250	775	853	920	1332
			500	1463	1573	1668	2250
			750	2135	2270	2386	3100
			1000	2801	2956	3090	3914
3.00	.50	100	1	16	23	29	66
			5	43	58	72	154
			10	68	90	109	225
			20	110	141	168	333
			30	149	187	220	421
			50	220	269	312	572
			75	304	364	416	735
			100	384	454	514	882
			250	838	948	1043	1625
			500	1551	1706	1840	2664
			750	2243	2434	2598	3607
			1000	2925	3145	3335	4500

Value of Variables (Monthly Base)			REORDER POINT BY ALLOWED STOCK OUT PERCENTAGE				
P	L	Q	S	20%	10%	5%	0%
3.00	1.00	1	1	3	4	4	8
			5	13	14	15	23
			10	24	26	27	38
			20	45	48	51	65
			30	67	70	73	91
			50	109	113	117	140
			75	160	166	170	199
			100	212	218	224	257
			250	519	529	537	589
			500	1027	1041	1053	1126
			750	1533	1550	1565	1655
			1000	2038	2058	2075	2179
3.00	1.00	10	1	6	8	9	20
			5	19	23	27	50
			10	32	38	44	77
			20	57	66	73	120
			30	81	92	101	158
			50	127	141	153	226
			75	183	200	215	305
			100	238	258	275	379
			250	560	591	618	783
			500	1085	1129	1167	1400
			750	1604	1658	1705	1990
			1000	2120	2182	2236	2566
3.00	1.00	50	1	11	15	19	42
			5	29	39	47	99
			10	47	61	73	146
			20	78	98	115	219
			30	107	131	151	279
			50	160	191	218	383
			75	224	262	295	496
			100	285	329	367	600
			250	634	704	764	1132
			500	1190	1288	1373	1894
			750	1733	1853	1957	2595
			1000	2269	2408	2528	3265
3.00	1.00	100	1	14	20	26	59
			5	37	51	63	136
			10	58	78	95	199
			20	94	122	146	293
			30	126	160	189	370
			50	185	229	267	500
			75	254	308	355	640
			100	320	382	436	766
			250	690	788	873	1394
			500	1269	1408	1528	2265
			750	1829	2000	2147	3049
			1000	2380	2577	2747	3789

Value of Variables (Monthly Base)				REORDER POINT BY ALLOWED STOCK OUT PERCENTAGE			
P	L	Q	S	20%	10%	5%	0%
6.00	0	1	1	8	9	10	16
			5	35	37	39	52
			10	67	70	73	91
			20	129	134	138	164
			30	191	197	202	234
			50	315	322	329	369
			75	468	477	485	535
			100	621	632	641	698
			250	1533	1550	1565	1655
			500	3047	3071	3091	3219
			750	4557	4587	4612	4768
			1000	6066	6100	6129	6310
6.00	0	10	1	13	16	19	37
			5	45	52	59	99
			10	81	92	101	158
			20	149	165	178	259
			30	216	235	251	350
			50	347	371	391	519
			75	507	537	562	718
			100	666	700	729	910
			250	1604	1658	1705	1990
			500	3147	3223	3289	3693
			750	4680	4774	4854	5349
			1000	6208	6316	6409	6980
6.00	0	50	1	21	28	35	75
			5	63	80	95	185
			10	107	131	151	279
			20	186	220	249	430
			30	261	302	338	559
			50	404	458	505	790
			75	578	644	701	1050
			100	747	823	889	1293
			250	1733	1853	1957	2595
			500	3329	3500	3647	4549
			750	4903	5112	5292	6397
			1000	6466	6707	6915	8191
6.00	0	100	1	27	38	47	104
			5	77	101	121	249
			10	126	160	189	370
			20	213	261	303	558
			30	294	353	404	717
			50	447	523	589	993
			75	630	724	804	1299
			100	808	916	1009	1580
			250	1829	2000	2147	3049
			500	3466	3707	3915	5191
			750	5070	5365	5620	7183
			1000	6658	6999	7294	9098

Value of Variables (Monthly Base)				REORDER POINT BY ALLOWED STOCK OUT PERCENTAGE			
P	L	Q	S	20%	10%	5%	0%
6.00	.50	1	1	7	9	9	15
			5	32	34	36	48
			10	61	65	67	85
			20	119	124	128	152
			30	176	182	186	216
			50	289	296	303	341
			75	430	439	446	494
			100	570	580	589	644
			250	1407	1423	1437	1523
			500	2795	2818	2838	2960
			750	4180	4208	4232	4382
			1000	5563	5596	5624	5797
6.00	.50	10	1	12	15	18	35
			5	42	49	55	94
			10	75	85	94	149
			20	138	153	165	243
			30	200	217	233	327
			50	320	343	363	485
			75	467	495	520	669
			100	613	646	674	847
			250	1475	1526	1571	1844
			500	2891	2964	3027	3413
			750	4298	4387	4464	4937
			1000	5699	5803	5892	6438
6.00	.50	50	1	20	27	33	72
			5	59	75	89	176
			10	100	123	143	265
			20	173	206	234	407
			30	242	282	317	528
			50	375	426	471	744
			75	535	598	652	987
			100	691	764	827	1213
			250	1598	1713	1813	2424
			500	3065	3228	3369	4233
			750	4511	4711	4883	5942
			1000	5946	6176	6376	7598
6.00	.50	100	1	25	36	45	99
			5	72	95	115	237
			10	118	151	179	352
			20	199	245	285	530
			30	274	331	380	679
			50	416	489	552	938
			75	585	675	752	1225
			100	749	853	942	1488
			250	1690	1853	1994	2858
			500	3196	3426	3626	4848
			750	4671	4954	5198	6694
			1000	6130	6457	6739	8466

Value of Variables (Monthly Base)				REORDER POINT BY ALLOWED STOCK OUT PERCENTAGE			
P	L	Q	S	20%	10%	5%	0%
6.00	1.00	1	1	7	8	9	14
			5	29	31	33	45
			10	56	59	62	78
			20	109	113	117	140
			30	160	166	170	199
			50	263	270	276	313
			75	391	400	407	452
			100	519	529	537	589
			250	1280	1296	1309	1391
			500	2543	2565	2584	2700
			750	3802	3829	3852	3995
			1000	5060	5091	5118	5283
6.00	1.00	10	1	11	14	17	33
			5	38	45	51	88
			10	69	79	87	139
			20	127	141	153	226
			30	183	200	215	305
			50	293	315	334	450
			75	427	454	477	620
			100	560	591	618	783
			250	1345	1394	1437	1697
			500	2634	2704	2764	3132
			750	3915	4000	4073	4525
			1000	5190	5288	5373	5894
6.00	1.00	50	1	18	25	31	68
			5	55	71	84	166
			10	93	115	134	250
			20	160	191	218	383
			30	224	262	295	496
			50	345	394	437	697
			75	491	552	604	923
			100	634	704	764	1132
			250	1463	1573	1668	2250
			500	2801	2956	3090	3914
			750	4118	4309	4473	5482
			1000	5425	5645	5835	7000
6.00	1.00	100	1	24	34	42	94
			5	68	90	109	225
			10	110	141	168	333
			20	185	229	267	500
			30	254	308	355	640
			50	384	454	514	882
			75	540	625	698	1150
			100	690	788	873	1394
			250	1551	1706	1840	2664
			500	2925	3145	3335	4500
			750	4271	4540	4773	6199
			1000	5601	5912	6181	7828

Value of Variables (Monthly Base)			REORDER POINT BY ALLOWED STOCK OUT PERCENTAGE				
P	L	Q	S	20%	10%	5%	0%
6.00	3.00	1	1	4	5	6	10
			5	18	20	21	30
			10	35	37	39	52
			20	67	70	73	91
			30	98	102	106	128
			50	160	166	170	199
			75	238	244	250	285
			100	315	322	329	369
			250	773	785	796	860
			500	1533	1550	1565	1655
			750	2290	2311	2329	2440
			1000	3047	3071	3091	3219
6.00	3.00	10	1	8	10	12	25
			5	25	31	35	64
			10	45	52	59	99
			20	81	92	101	158
			30	116	129	140	210
			50	183	200	215	305
			75	265	286	304	415
			100	347	371	391	519
			250	824	862	895	1096
			500	1604	1658	1705	1990
			750	2378	2444	2501	2850
			1000	3147	3223	3289	3693
6.00	3.00	50	1	13	19	23	52
			5	38	50	61	125
			10	63	80	95	185
			20	107	131	151	279
			30	147	177	202	358
			50	224	262	295	496
			75	315	362	402	649
			100	404	458	505	790
			250	915	1000	1073	1525
			500	1733	1853	1957	2595
			750	2535	2683	2810	3592
			1000	3329	3500	3647	4549
6.00	3.00	100	1	18	25	32	72
			5	48	65	80	170
			10	77	101	121	249
			20	126	160	189	370
			30	171	212	248	469
			50	254	308	355	640
			75	353	419	476	825
			100	447	523	589	993
			250	983	1103	1207	1845
			500	1829	2000	2147	3049
			750	2653	2862	3042	4147
			1000	3466	3707	3915	5191

The following appeared in FINANCIAL EXECUTIVE Magazine following publication of a condensed version of this book in the April 1964 edition. It is reprinted here because it expands on the original article.

Excerpt From FINANCIAL EXECUTIVE (September, 1964)

Re: "Principles of Inventory Management" by Arthur Snyder in the April 1964 issue of FINANCIAL EXECUTIVE, pp. 19-20. The section on quantity discounts leaves me wondering. Let us compare the total yearly costs of the company that buys at the computed EOQ (34) with those of the company that buys in lots of (100) where the price is lowest.

Order size	34	100
Orders per year	35	12
Price at order quantity	$10.80	$7.20
Value of order	$367.00	$720.00
Extra value	-	$353.00
Average extra	-	$177.00[1]
Interest cost @ 24%	-	$42.00
Cost of orders (@ 1.20)	$42.00	$14.00
Cost of years use (1200)	$13,000.00	$8,600.00
Total cost	$13,042.00	$8,656.00
Saving in buying in lots of 100		$4,386.00

[1]Average extra amount of money that would be invested.

R. P. HAYNES
Controller
Berg Electronics, Inc.
New Cumberland, PA

The Author Responds:

Dear Mr. Haynes:

Your question concerning the application of the EOQ Formula to purchase quantities involving quantity discounts is well taken. The procedure recommended in the article is not correct. The EOQ can be used, as illustrated, provided there is no applicable quantity discount. The approach must be modified, however, if the unit price is a function of a quantity discount.

I have attached a revision of that portion of the article pertaining to the application of the EOQ to quantity discounts, which provides a procedure which clearly analyzes a situation involving quantity discounts.

Thank you for calling this to our attention and if you have any further comments, I would certainly appreciate hearing from you.

ARTHUR SNYDER

The Editors of FINANCIAL EXECUTIVE Add Their Note:

Our constant concern is whether the articles are of interest to the readers and, when we see a response (as there was to this article), we feel that we are close to target. Mr. Snyder has also apprised us of the fact that there had been over 300 requests for the booklet covering an analysis of the derivation of the OP equation mentioned on page 14 of the April issue.

Among the requests were letters that testified further to the usefulness of our articles; (From a controller): *"You have introduced a number of very novel (at least to me) ideas, which I intend to introduce in our company."* (From a manager, Audit Division, Controller's Department): *"I should like to make a more detailed study of the concepts advanced."* (From a manager, Production & Inventory Planning): *"I read with a great deal of interest your article... we also utilize the Poisson distribution as a basis for establishing safety stock. We also advocate the use of an economic order quantity range, although not in so formal a manner as indicated in your article."* (From a member of a Data Planning Services Department*): "I read your excellent paper in a circulating copy of FINANCIAL EXECUTIVE. Are you also able to provide a reprint of the paper? The information is such that I would appreciate the availability of a copy in my files for ready reference."* (From a member of one of the "Big Eight" CPA concerns): *"You should be commended on your concise yet complete coverage of a very difficult subject."*

Of interest to us also was the fact that there were requests from a university in Australia and a large oil company in Panama. Mr. Snyder ends his note to us with *"Distribution of FINANCIAL EXECUTIVE seems worldwide as I have had requests from England and Canada as well."*

MR. SNYDER'S REVISED TEXT

Occasionally you will hear a purchasing agent or distributor ask the question: "The EOQ formula is fine for advising how much to make, but can we use it to determine how much to buy?" The answer to this question is a very definite, "Yes."

$$EOQ = \sqrt{\frac{2SO}{RU}}$$

S = Sales or usage
R = Investment factor
O = Ordering costs
U = Unit costs

The EOQ formula shown above is applicable to both manufacturing and purchasing situations. The Appendix (pages 20-21 of the April 1964 issue) provides a thorough analysis of how each variable used in the EOQ equation is evaluated depending upon whether the item is manufactured or purchased.

Assume that a company has an annual usage of 100 units of Item A which has a purchase price of $50.00 per unit. The company has an established procedure for determining optimum purchase quantities based on the use of the EOQ formula and the following data are applicable to Item A:

Investment Factor (R) = 15% per year
Ordering Costs (O) = $5.00 per order
Unit Costs (U) = Purchase price per unit plus 10% for inventory carrying costs.

Based on the foregoing data, the economic order quantity (EOQ) is 11 units which is determined as follows:

$$EOQ = \sqrt{\frac{2SO}{RU}} = \sqrt{\frac{2 \times 100 \times 5}{.15 \times 55}} = 11 \text{ units}$$

QUANTITY DISCOUNT

A common practice in industry today is the "quantity discount" which is used to encourage buyers to place larger orders. Many suppliers offer a discount schedule wherein the discount increases with the number of units ordered. The result is a variable unit cost for the item which is dependent on the quantity ordered. This problem does not exist for the manufacturer as his unit cost (U) can usually be considered constant. This brings us to the question, "How is the quantity discount and the resulting variable unit cost recognized in determining the EOQ for purchased items?"

The procedure for determining the economic order quantity for an item whose net purchase price is based on a quantity discount schedule involves two steps:

The first step is to calculate the EOQ for each unit cost provided by the quantity discount schedule. The suggested order quantity will be the largest EOQ provided it falls within the quantity range upon which the unit cost and respective discount is based.

The second step is to calculate the Unit Purchase Cost (UPC) for the item if purchased in lot sizes of the suggested order quantity and compare it with the UPC if purchased at quantities which permit the higher quantity discount. The minimum UPC is the economic order quantity. To illustrate this procedure, let us use the following example:

STEP I

Assume that Item A can be purchased according to the following quantity discount schedule: (Unit Cost (U)* = Net purchase price per unit *plus* 10% for inventory carrying costs). (Schedule 1)

Based on the above data, we can calculate the respective EOQs for the three unit costs (U, Schedule 2) provided by the discount schedule.

Same issue with this table: tabs used in order to simplify production (but they make proofing a bit more difficult.)

Schedule 1:

Purchase Quantity	Discount	Net Purchase Price per Unit	Unit Cost (U)*
(a) 1-9	—	$50.00	$55.00
(b) 10-99	10%	$45.00	$49.50
(c) 100+	15%	$42.50	$46.75

Schedule 2:

	(a)	(b)	(c)
Purchase Quantity	1-9	10-99	100+
Unit Cost (U)	$55.00	$49.50	$46.75
Annual Sales (S)	100	100	100
Investment Factor (R)	15%	15%	15%
Ordering Costs (O)	$5.00	$5.00	$5.00
EOQ	11	12*	12

Schedule 3:

	(b)	(c)
Purchase Quantity	12	100
Purchase Price per Unit	$45.00	$42.50
Purchase Cost for 100 units	$4500	$4250
Inventory Carrying Cost @ 10%	450	425
Ordering Costs	40	5
Total Purchase Cost	$4990	$4680

As shown below, the indicated economic order quantity (*) is 12 units as it is the largest EOQ which falls within its respective purchase quantity range (10-99 units).

STEP II

As shown below, if we purchase Item A in lot sizes of 12 units, we will have a total purchase cost of $4990. However, if we purchase in lot sizes of 100 in order to obtain the higher quantity discount, we effect a savings of $310 as the total purchase cost is only $4680. Obviously, there is no advantage in considering a lot size of less than 100 units. (Schedule 3)

The problem to resolve, therefore, is: "Is the investment in a purchase order quantity of 100 units which provides a one-year supply of Item A justified by the annual savings of $310?" To answer this question we must calculate the Unit Purchase Cost (UPC) for each condition. The UPC equation is fully discussed in Appendix H (page 77) and can be stated as follows:

$$UPC = U + \frac{UNR}{2S} + \frac{O}{N} + \frac{OR}{2N}$$

Substitution of the data for each condition into this equation provides us with the following UPC for Item A if purchased in lot sizes of 12 and 100 units:

Purchase Quantity (N)
Unit Cost (U)
Investment Factor (R)
Ordering Costs (O)
Sales or Usage (S)
Unit Purchase Cost (UPC)

(b)	(c)
12	100
$49.50	$46.75
15%	15%
$5.00	$5.00
100	100
$50.39	$50.31

As shown above, the UPC for Item A if purchased in lot sizes of 100 is $50.31 or eight cents less than the UPC if purchased in lot sizes of 12 units. The net savings, therefore, by purchasing in lot sizes of 100 units is $8.00 per year. As a matter of interest, it would not be economical to purchase in lot sizes of 100 units if the annual sales or usage(s) was only 75 units. On the other hand, if sales were 200 units per year, the annual savings would exceed $300.

Conclusions

It should be noted that the most important factor in evaluating the Economic Ordering Quantity for an item whose net purchase price is based on a quantity discount schedule is the Investment Factor (R). If the Investment Factor is assigned a value of zero, then the optimum purchase quantity will always be an amount to permit the maximum quantity discount. The Investment Factor, however, can seldom be considered as having a value of zero as its function is to provide a rate of return on the inventory investment which is commensurate with the risks and costs associated with the particular business. Normally, the Investment Factor will vary from six per cent to 15 per cent depending on the type of product, degree of risk involved (such as product obsolescence), and working capital requirements.

Step II of the foregoing procedure was shown. for those who wish to apply an exact and rigorous method to the determination of an EOQ for purchased items, the net price for which is determined by a quantity discount schedule. It may not always be convenient or necessary to use this procedure. On purchased items where the annual usage involves a significant investment, it is probably advisable to review each of these items individually using the previously described method. The majority of purchased items, however, usually involve a small investment and the choice of the proper quantity discount can be estimated by comparing (a) the annual savings in purchase price and ordering costs if the order quantity is increased to the next quantity discount bracket to (b) the annual cost of the added investment. If the annual savings exceed the annual cost, then you are justified in increasing your order quantity to obtain the higher quantity discount.

Using the data from the previous example, we would calculate thus:

Annual Savings = In Purchase Price + In Ordering Costs
= 100 ($49.50 — $46.75) + $5.00 (8 — I)
= $275 + $35
= $310

Annual Cost = Investment Factor X Average Added Investment
= 15% x ½ (100 x $46.75 — 12 x $49.50)
= $306

The above "short-cut method" for Step II supports the previous conclusion that it is economical to purchase Item A in lot sizes of 100 units.

Derivation Of The Unit Purchase Cost (Upc) Equation For Purchase Quantities Involving Quantity Discounts

The purpose of the UNIT PURCHASE COST (UPC) equation is to permit the calculation of the average annual cost per unit of an item which can be purchased according to a quantity discount schedule. The derivation of the UPC Equation assumes that the purchase quantity (N) does not exceed one year's supply and the inventory is depleted at a uniform rate before a reorder is issued. The variables used in the derivation of the equation are:

S = Sales or Usage
O = Ordering Costs
U = Unit Costs
N = Purchase Quantity
R = Investment Factor

The above variables are carefully discussed and defined in Appendix A (pages 20-21 FINANCIAL EXECUTIVE, April 1964). The derivation of the UPC equation is as follows:

1) The return required on the averaged investment per unit can be stated as follows:

$$\frac{N \times U}{2} \times \frac{R}{S} = \frac{NUR}{2S}$$

2) The ordering costs per unit is:

$$\frac{S}{N} \times \frac{O}{S} = \frac{O}{N}$$

3) The return required on the average investment in ordering costs per unit is:

$$\frac{O}{N} \times \frac{R}{2} = \frac{OR}{2N}$$

4) The Unit Purchase Cost (UPC) equation is therefore:

$$UPC = U + \frac{NUR}{2S} + \frac{O}{N} + \frac{OR}{2N}$$

www.ingramcontent.com/pod-product-compliance
Lightning Source LLC
Chambersburg PA
CBHW081218170526
45165CB00009B/2860